HOW TO BEAT THE 80/20 RULE IN SELLING

Why Most Salespeople Don't Perform and What to Do About It

Second Edition

ALAN RIGG

How to Beat the 80/20 Rule in Selling

Published by Hats Off Books
610 East Delano Street, Suite 104
Tucson, AZ 85705, USA
www.hatsoffbooks.com

Publisher's Cataloging-in-Publication Data
(Provided by Quality Books, Inc.)

Rigg, Alan.
   How to beat the 80/20 rule in selling : why most salespeople don't perform and what to do about it / Alan Rigg. -- 2nd ed.
      p. cm.
   Includes bibliographical references and index.
   LCCN 2004091030
   ISBN 1-587-36313-5

   1. Selling.   I. Title

HF5438.25.R54 2004   658.85
                         QBI04-200130

CONTENTS

INTRODUCTION

This book was written to serve three audiences. The first audience is individuals who are considering the question, "I wonder if I have what it takes to succeed in sales?" The second audience is business owners, executives, and managers who come from non-sales backgrounds and want to understand selling and sales management better. The third audience is sales-savvy business owners, executives, and managers who are struggling with the question, "Why is it that a just a small fraction of my company's salespeople produce the bulk of our sales?"

There are hundreds of books that have been written about sales. What is so special about this one? First, most books about sales are written from the standpoint of teaching someone *how* to sell. They don't address the question of whether someone *should* pursue a career in sales. Second, information about selling and sales management is *fragmented*. If you take the time to read a lot of books, listen to a lot of tapes, and attend a lot of classes, you can build a broad base of knowledge...eventually. This book consolidates much of that information into one place. Third, despite the fact that companies spend *billions* of dollars annually to recruit and train salespeople, the majority leave, are terminated, or turn out to be mediocre producers. Clearly there are missing pieces to the sales puzzle. This book identifies the missing pieces.

How to Beat the 80/20 Rule in Selling is not based upon "ivory tower" research conducted by academics who have never sold for a living. I have personally made the transition from a career in finance to a career in sales. I learned how to sell successfully, and continue to make a handsome living from sales. I even founded a company, 80/20 Performance, Inc., to help others beat the 80/20 Rule in selling. I have *lived* the contents of this book, and continue to live them every single day.

Some Personal History

Back in 1985, I was fed up with my budding career in finance. I had a good job and worked for a great company (General Electric). There was just one problem. My everyday work bored me stiff!

As I considered making a career change, I explored what various friends and acquaintances did for a living. Like many people, I was attracted to some of the benefits I perceived in a career in sales. Salespeople can make a lot of money. They can have a lot of control over their schedule. They get to meet a lot of interesting people. And, they seem to have a lot of fun! I knew I didn't know *how* to sell, but I figured I could learn. So, I bought some books and tapes and started looking for a sales job.

Finding my first sales job was pretty easy. There were plenty of entry-level sales jobs listed in the classified ads in the newspaper. I made some phone calls and faxed some resumes. Within a couple of weeks I landed a job selling typesetting accessories and supplies. My new employer even offered a three-week sales training program. Surely I had found my path to sales success!

I failed in that job. Unfortunately, the "sales training" program that my employer offered focused more on product knowledge than it did on selling skills. I studied hard, and even skipped a big night out with my classmates the evening before our "final exam." My diligence didn't help much, though. While I managed to pass the exam, when I went back to the office I didn't sell very much. Fortunately my employer decided to move my department to another state before anyone decided to fire me. Since I didn't want to move, they laid me off and generously gave me a month's pay as severance.

Armed with a whopping six months of sales experience, I started searching for another sales job. Within two weeks, I landed a position selling dictation equipment. Now, instead of telephone sales, I was doing "field sales." Another step forward, and with more sales training to boot!

I failed in that job, too. However, good fortune intervened once again. During a cold call I met a gentleman who ran a small sales training company. He and I hit it off, and he expressed interest in hiring me. He invited me to attend a training session he was conducting over the weekend, and I accepted the invitation. Attending that training session turned out to be the pivotal point in my sales career.

During the training session I was introduced to a number of concepts that had never been mentioned in the books I had read, the tapes I had listened to, or the "sales training" classes I had attended. I learned that there are different selling styles, and that each style requires different capabilities. I was also exposed to the basics of consultative selling, which turned out to be the style for which I am best suited.

I decided to join the sales training company. In thirty days I became ten times the salesperson I had been previously. Within ninety days I was teaching consultative selling skills and techniques. I even helped clients hire consultative salespeople and sales managers and mentored these new hires in the field.

Unfortunately, there was one fly in the ointment. My boss was truly an exceptional salesperson, trainer, and mentor, but he wasn't as talented at running a business. I eventually got tired of holding paychecks and decided to go find a consultative sales job.

After considerable research I decided that I wanted to work for a national computer distributor. I secured an interview with the manager of the local sales office and we spent two hours dissecting his business. I used all of my consultative selling skills during that interview. I asked relevant, insightful questions and used the answers to construct additional questions. It was a great interview, and we both thoroughly enjoyed it. The only downside was that the manager didn't have any field sales openings. Since I really wanted to work for his company, I made an alternative proposal. I felt I could add value by prospecting for additional leads for the existing salespeople. The manager agreed, and hired me to do just that.

For four months I dialed and smiled, and uncovered leads that generated an incremental $500,000 in sales. At the end of the four months, the manager fired an underperforming salesperson and promoted me to field sales. I made my quota during my first full year in the job and produced 228 percent of quota during my second year. A promotion to sales management followed shortly thereafter.

During the 1990s I had the opportunity to view sales from a variety of managerial perspectives, including sales management, sales support management, materials management, business process improvement, training, and executive management. My curiosity was piqued by the imbalance I repeatedly observed in performance across sales teams.

How inconsistent is sales performance in most companies? The title of this book refers to an 80/20 ratio. When this ratio applies to a sales team, it means that 80 percent of the company's sales are produced by just 20 percent of the company's salespeople. Conversely, the other 80 percent of the company's salespeople produce just 20 percent of the company's sales. In some companies the ratio is 75/25, 70/30, 60/40, or even 90/10. Regardless of the actual ratio, the problem it describes is still the same: *the vast majority of the salespeople on most sales teams produce a fraction of what the top producers on the very same sales teams produce.*

How can this be? Aren't all of the salespeople in a company hired using the *same* recruiting process? Don't they work for the *same* company? Aren't they selling the *same* offerings to the *same* types of customers? Don't they have access to the *same* training and support resources? If all these things are the same, then why do salespeople perform so differently?

Defining the Real Problem

Many years ago my engineer father told me, "If you want to solve a problem, the first thing you have to do is figure out what the *real problem* is." I applied this advice to the problem of inconsistent sales performance. I thought about the processes that most companies use to hire, train, and manage salespeople, and realized that the failure rate of these processes is nothing short of spectacular. How so? In companies that are struggling with the 80/20 Rule, the same processes that produce the occasional superstar salesperson are *four times more likely* to produce mediocre salespeople or complete washouts.

However, process failures are not the real problem. I knew I needed to look deeper to find the causes of these failures. So, I began trying to separate the *subjective* (based upon opinion) information that companies gather when hiring, training, and managing salespeople from *objective* (based upon fact) information. That is when the real problem came into clear focus.

The real problem is, most of the processes that companies use to hire, train, and manage salespeople are based almost entirely upon *subjective* information. Consider some examples. What are resumes? They are an individual's *subjective* portrayal of their capabilities and experiences. What occurs during an interview? Interviewees attempt to package their responses to questions in a manner that will make the best *impression*. Meanwhile, interviewers are forming *personal opinions* about candidates' qualifications for the position.

I'm not suggesting that subjective information is useless. Subjective information is a valid and valuable component of any "people decision." However, if decisions based solely upon subjective information produce an undesirable result 80 percent of the time (remember the 80/20 Rule?), doesn't it make sense to consider making a change?

Adding Objective Information to "People Decisions"

How can companies add objective information to the processes they use to hire, train and manage salespeople? One way is to take advantage of modern assessment technologies. This doesn't mean behavioral tests or personality profiles. While these instruments can help improve understanding and communication, they are not very effective for matching individuals to jobs and predicting performance. The modern assessment technologies I'm referring to identify the rate at which an individual learns, their problem-solving abilities, the interests that motivate and gratify them, and selected behavioral traits.

When modern assessment technologies are used to assess top performers in a particular sales job, and lesser performers in the same sales job, the attributes that differentiate the top performers can be isolated. Armed with this information, companies can assess job applicants to determine how well they stack up against known top performers. If a job applicant's assessment scores are similar to the scores for known top performers, it is likely the job applicant will perform in a fashion similar to the top performers.

Modern assessment technologies can also be used to identify individualized training needs for existing salespeople. How? The assessment results for underperforming salespeople can be compared to the results for top performers. The differences can be analyzed to determine whether it is reasonable to expect training to impact the salesperson's performance. If training is warranted, a *highly targeted* training curriculum can be developed for each salesperson. Targeted training usually produces a much greater impact on performance than generalized training curriculums.

So, is this a book about assessments? Not at all! This book explores a variety of topics that will boost your understanding of both selling and sales management. Key topics include: why salespeople perform differently, the attributes required for sales success, relationship preferences and selling styles, recruiting myths, the impact of sales manager style, how to develop an effective prospecting plan, the secret to closing more sales, forecasting and pipeline management, how to assign sales territories, how to develop an effective compensation plan, and why most sales training programs fail.

Do these topics sound interesting to you? Good! Turn the page and let's get started!

CHAPTER 1

THE 80/20 RULE

What is "the 80/20 Rule"?

The concept of "the 80/20 Rule" is widely recognized. However, that does not mean it is *universally* recognized. Why don't we take a minute to ensure that we have a common understanding of this important concept?

The 80/20 Rule originated with an Italian economist named Vilfredo Pareto, who studied the distribution of wealth in a variety of countries around 1900. Pareto concluded that there was a predictable imbalance in the distribution of wealth, with approximately 80 percent of the wealth in most countries controlled by approximately 20 percent of the people. This observation eventually became known as "Pareto's Principle" or "the 80/20 Rule."

Today, the 80/20 Rule is used to describe any scenario where the majority of results come from a minority of inputs or participants.

What is the Financial Impact of the 80/20 Rule?

When the 80/20 Rule applies to a company's sales team, both revenues and expenses are impacted. We will explore these impacts separately.

Revenue Impact

The revenue impact can be demonstrated using a simple example. Let's assume that Sample Company has ten salespeople, and annual sales for the company are $10 million. If the 80/20 Rule applies to Sample Company's sales force, here is how annual sales are distributed:

Table 1: 80/20 Sales Distribution

Percentage	Number of Salespeople	Annual Sales (Each Salesperson)	Total Sales
Top 20%	2	$4,000,000	$8,000,000
Other 80%	8	250,000	2,000,000
TOTALS	10		$10,000,000

Twenty percent of ten salespeople equals two salespeople (10 x 0.20). These two salespeople generate 80 percent of Sample Company's sales, or $8 million ($10 million x 0.80). Divide $8 million by the two salespeople, and the revenue per salesperson is $4 million.

Similar calculations can be made for the remainder of Sample Company's sales force. Eighty percent of ten salespeople equals eight salespeople (10 x 0.80). These eight salespeople generate 20 percent of Sample Company's sales, or $2 million ($10 million x 0.20). Divide $2 million by eight salespeople, and the revenue per salesperson is $250,000.

Now, consider a couple of "what ifs." What if Sample Company increases the proportion of top performers on its sales team from 20 percent to 30 percent? Here is the revenue impact of this change:

Table 2: 70/30 Sales Distribution

Percentage	Number of Salespeople	Annual Sales (Each Salesperson)	Total Sales
Top 30%	3	$4,000,000	$12,000,000
Other 70%	7	250,000	1,750,000
TOTAL	10		$13,750,000

By replacing one of its lesser-performing salespeople with one additional top performer (10 percent of the sales team), Sample Company increases its total revenue by 37.5 percent!

What if Sample Company increases the proportion of top performers on its sales team from 20 percent to 40 percent? Here is the revenue impact of this change:

Table 3: 60/40 Sales Distribution

Percentage	Number of Salespeople	Annual Sales (Each Salesperson)	Total Sales
Top 40%	4	$4,000,000	$16,000,000
Other 60%	6	250,000	1,500,000
TOTALS	10		$17,500,000

By replacing two lesser performers with two top performers (20 percent of the sales team), Sample Company increases its total revenue by a whopping 75 percent!

Expense Impact

Clearly, increasing the proportion of top performers on a sales team beneficially impacts revenue. However, increasing the proportion of top performers also beneficially impacts expenses. Why? Because there is usually less turnover among top sales performers than there is among lesser performers. When turnover is reduced, companies don't need to invest as much time and money in recruiting, selecting, and training new salespeople.

Bottom Line Impact

The bottom line impact of increasing the ratio of top performers on a sales team can be summarized with the following equation:

HIGHER REVENUES
- LOWER EXPENSES
= INCREA$ED PROFIT$

CHAPTER 2

WHY DO SALESPEOPLE PERFORM DIFFERENTLY?

In their book *Now, Discover Your Strengths,* Marcus Buckingham and Donald O. Clifton report that great managers and average managers have different expectations for their employees. According to Buckingham and Clifton, average managers assume that "each person can learn to be competent in almost anything," while great managers assume that "each person's talents are enduring and unique."

Most sales books and sales training programs seem to share the "average manager" point of view. In other words, they seem to assume that *anyone* can learn to be competent in sales. All that is required is the investment of time and effort in learning a particular set of skills. Once you learn these skills, you are on your way to sales success.

Unfortunately, this approach does not work for everyone. How many salespeople do you know who are struggling to make quota? Why are they struggling? Is it the state of the economy? (If other individuals on the same sales team are making their numbers, blaming the economy won't earn much sympathy.) Is it because they don't work hard enough? Is it because they don't have enough product knowledge? Do they need to work harder on their sales skills? Do they need more coaching from their managers?

What if the "great manager" point of view is correct? What if everyone *cannot* become proficient in sales? What if success in sales requires a *unique* set of talents?

Herb Greenberg, Harold Weinstein, and Patrick Sweeney report this very conclusion in their book, *How to Hire and Develop Your Next Top Performer: The Five Qualities That Make Salespeople Great*. After correlating hundreds of thousands of assessments that were conducted over several decades with actual sales performance measurements, they conclude, "Fifty-five percent of the people earning their living in sales should be doing something else" and "another 20 to 25 percent have what it takes to sell, but they should be selling something else."

If unique talents are indeed required for sales success, what process can companies use to identify which talents are critical? Once these critical talents have been identified, how can companies determine whether individual salespeople and sales candidates have these talents?

The tools and processes that many companies use to source and select salespeople do not address these questions. Consider the following examples:

1. **Employment Ads:** Many employment ads list a variety of "knockout factors" such as

required skills, education, and experience. The purpose of these knockout factors is to screen out undesirable candidates. However, is there really a correlation between specific knockout factors and an individual's ability to sell? If 80 percent of a company's sales force produces just 20 percent of its sales, how good a job are that company's knockout factors doing of screening out unqualified candidates? Might they actually be screening out *qualified* candidates instead?

2. **Resumes:** Resumes are purely subjective documents. They are written with the specific intention of portraying an individual's skills and experiences in the best possible light. Do some people misrepresent their qualifications on their resumes? Absolutely! However, even if the information on a resume is completely accurate, what correlation does it have with that individual's ability to sell *your* company's offering?

3. **Interviews:** The accuracy of the interview process is also suspect. As Lou Adler explains in his book, *Hire With Your Head*, "More errors are made in the first 30 minutes of the interview than any other time. Emotions, biases, perceptions, stereotypes, and first impressions

are powerful human forces that profoundly affect individual judgment."

What do these three examples have in common? They all describe tools and processes that are completely reliant upon *subjective* information.

There is nothing inherently wrong with using subjective information to make "people decisions." In fact, subjective information should play an important role in *every* people decision. However, if a company is struggling with the 80/20 Rule in its sales organization, clearly its current process isn't working as well as the company would like. Something needs to change. One useful change would be the addition of *objective* information to the "people decision" process.

How can companies acquire objective information about salespeople and sales candidates? One of the easiest ways is through the use of modern assessment technologies. Extensive research and validation studies have shown these technologies to be very effective at matching people to jobs and predicting performance.

If a company chooses to assess its salespeople and sales candidates, what attributes should its managers look for in the assessment results? Which attributes are most responsible for sales success? The answers to these questions are provided in the next chapter.

CHAPTER 3

THE ATTRIBUTES REQUIRED FOR SALES SUCCESS

While all twelve of the attributes listed in this chapter impact sales performance, the first four attributes have the largest and most universal impact. Additionally, these four attributes can be used as core determinants for Relationship Preference and Selling Style, which are defined in Chapter 4.

Critical Attributes

1. **Sales Drive**: Does the individual enjoy presenting, persuading, negotiating, and motivating others? How *much* do they enjoy these activities?

An individual with a strong Sales Drive does not necessarily derive gratification solely from *closing* sales.

They also enjoy performing the *activities* that make up the sales process.

It is entirely possible for an individual to have too much Sales Drive. Have you ever dealt with an excessively pushy salesperson? This type of salesperson seems to feel that a "win-lose" transaction is acceptable...as long as it is the customer who is on the "lose" side of the equation. Most of us don't enjoy this type of sales experience very much.

2. **Emotional Toughness:** How rapidly does the individual rebound from rejection? Do they learn from their experiences and move on quickly? Or do they suffer a sustained reduction in productivity?

Emotional Toughness is especially important when a sales job requires significant prospecting, as rejection is an unavoidable component of this activity. If a salesperson cannot rebound rapidly from rejection, they will have difficulty prospecting effectively.

3. **Reasoning Ability:** Does the individual ask good questions? Can they dissect answers and pick out the pieces that will help them advance the conversation toward a desired end result?

The Consultative Sales Style (discussed in Chapter 4) requires a strong Reasoning Ability. The salespeople that use this style must be able to ask prospects and customers questions, dissect the answers to identify possible needs, relate the needs to potential solutions, and plan additional questions. All of this occurs on the fly, while the prospect or customer is still talking.

4. Service Drive: How friendly and agreeable is the individual? How interested are they in building relationships and helping others?

We expect salespeople to be friendly, cooperative, and agreeable. Service Drive must be a *good* thing, right? Yes...but only to a point. If a salesperson has too much Service Drive, they tend to "give away the store." They are more concerned about being liked than they are about making sales or ensuring that they are managing *mutually* beneficial business relationships.

To be successful, salespeople need to be able to balance a customer's needs with the salesperson's own needs (to make sales) and their company's needs (to make a profit). This type of win-win-win scenario is the only kind of business relationship that can survive over the long term.

Other Important Attributes

The attributes listed below each play an important role in the achievement of sales success. However, the relative importance of each attribute differs based upon the unique requirements of each specific sales job.

5. Assertiveness: How self-assured is the individual? How effective are they at convincing others to take action?

Prospects and customers don't always feel comfortable making decisions, even when the decisions are in their own personal and professional best interests. Salespeople need to be Assertive enough to help their prospects and customers make it over decision-making humps.

6. **Attitude:** How positive is the individual's attitude? Do they perceive their glass to be half empty or half full?

A salesperson with a positive Attitude is able to bounce back from rejection, delays, and other sales challenges. They don't waste time trying to place blame. Instead, they focus on finding positive resolutions to issues and looking for opportunities to replicate these successes.

7. **Communication Skills:** How precisely does the individual communicate, both verbally and in writing? Are their communications clear and effective?

Strong Communication Skills are especially important when a sales position requires the salesperson to make frequent presentations and/or write compelling letters and proposals.

8. **Competitiveness:** How competitive is the individual? How does the individual's competitiveness manifest itself?

Competition can be a terrific motivator. However, it can also be taken to extremes. Excessively competitive salespeople may lose perspective and blindly pursue victory regardless of cost. This can lead to unprofitable sales, win-lose relationships with customers, and rocky relationships with suppliers, support personnel, and other sales team members.

9. **Energy:** How energetic is the individual? Are they always on the go, or do they need to be prodded into action?

High Energy is important for any sales role that requires significant prospecting activity. Plus, the level of Energy is often an indicator of whether a salesperson is *internally* motivated or *externally* motivated.

Salespeople with strong internal motivation rarely need to be prodded into action. A larger concern is that they may initiate action before they complete a plan of action (ready-shoot-aim). However, once a manager confirms that an internally motivated salesperson has a viable plan of action, they can rely on this salesperson to aggressively pursue the plan to completion with little further direction or encouragement.

Externally motivated salespeople require much more regular and frequent managerial attention than internally motivated salespeople. They may do excellent work when told what to do, when to do it, and how to do it. However, they need frequent direction and regular encouragement in order to maintain the desired level of productivity.

10. **Independence:** How readily does the individual accept direction from others?

Highly Independent salespeople prefer to do their work with as little direction (which they interpret as interference) from their manager as possible. Less Independent salespeople are more likely to need and appreciate frequent interaction with their manager.

11. **Learning Rate:** How rapidly does the individual learn new information? What styles of learning are most productive for them?

Learning Rate should be an important consideration when planning any type of sales training program. Why? Because different individuals learn at different rates. To better understand the impact of learning rates, consider this example. How quickly can you fill a one-gallon bucket versus a one-gallon milk jug? Both vessels have the same one-gallon capacity. However, because the milk jug has a much smaller opening, you are forced to fill it at a much slower rate

Now, apply this concept to a training situation. If slower learners and faster learners are placed in the same class, what is likely to happen? There are several possibilities. First, the teaching pace may satisfy the faster learners. However, the slower learners won't able to keep up. They will become frustrated and have a negative training experience. Second, the teaching pace may satisfy the slower learners. However, this pace will be too slow for the faster learners. They will become bored and have a negative training experience. Third, the teaching pace may be too fast for the slower learners, but too slow for the faster learners. *Both* groups will become frustrated and have a negative training experience!

12. **Tolerance for Administration:** How willing is the individual to perform administrative activities? How much attention do they pay to details?

Details? Don't all salespeople *hate* details? How can this attribute be important to sales success?

Actually, there are a number of sales roles that require attention to detail and a tolerance for administration. One example is the financial advisor who must comply with strict regulatory requirements. Another example is the salesperson who is responsible for increasing account penetration. Before they can increase account penetration, they need to conduct research to determine how much of their company's portfolio a customer is already buying. A third example is the salesperson who sells warranty renewals. This salesperson must examine historical records to determine when a customer's warranties expire, and what kinds of service upgrades and add-ons might be appropriate.

Tolerance for administration is also beneficial in any sales role where the salesperson is expected to submit accurate forecasts and update records in the company's CRM (Client Relationship Management) system in a timely fashion.

CHAPTER 4

RELATIONSHIP PREFERENCES AND SELLING STYLES

Not all sales jobs are created equal. They differ in terms of the type of relationship the salesperson develops with their customers and the selling style that is most effective.

There are any number of labels that can be used to define relationship preferences and selling styles. However, you should be able to categorize any sales job using the three relationship preferences and the four selling styles that are described in this chapter.

Relationship Preferences

There are three primary relationship preferences:

1. **Hunter:** Once the sale is made, this salesperson prefers to move on to new conquests.

2. **Farmer:** A Farmer calls upon existing customers with the intention of developing an ongo-

ing stream of business and maximizing account penetration.

NOTE: Account penetration consists of repeated, consistent efforts to sell a company's *entire portfolio* of products and services to a customer, and expand the sales relationship to all of a customer's divisions and business units.

3. **Hybrid:** This salesperson is effective at creating new sales relationships and deepening relationships after the initial sale is made.

To develop a deeper understanding of these three relationship preferences, consider how the weightings differ for the four critical attributes for sales success. This information is summarized in Table 4

**Table 4: Relationship Preference
and Critical Attributes**

	Sales Drive	Emotional Toughness	Reasoning Ability	Service Drive
Hunter	High	High	High/ Medium/Low	Low
Farmer	High/ Medium	Medium/Low	High/ Medium	High/ Medium
Hybrid	High/ Medium	High/ Medium	High/ Medium	High/ Medium

The *Hunter* role is focused on finding and securing new sales relationships. Once a new customer has been secured, the Hunter prefers to hand off the customer to another salesperson (a Farmer) for ongoing service. The

Hunter will then go pursue additional new sales relationships.

In order for salespeople to be successful Hunters, they need a strong Sales Drive. This means they derive considerable satisfaction from persuading others and the activities involved in selling. Most Hunters also prospect aggressively. This requires them to possess a high level of Emotional Toughness in order to deal effectively with rejection. If the Hunter's sales style is Consultative or Relationship (these styles are discussed later in this chapter), a strong Reasoning Ability can be valuable. A strong Service Drive is not necessary for most Hunters, especially if their employer allows them to hand off new customers to other salespeople for ongoing service.

The *Farmer* does not secure many new customers. This sales role is focused on deepening and broadening existing customer relationships. When Farmers do secure new customers, it is often the result of referrals from existing customers. In a pure Hunter/Farmer model, Farmers may hand off these referrals to Hunters.

Some Farmers have a very strong Sales Drive and use it to their advantage. However, since most Farmers do not spend a lot of time pursuing new sales relationships, a strong Sales Drive is not a requirement. (Farmers *do* need to have a strong enough Sales Drive to be comfortable asking for orders and pursuing add-on business.) Because most of their conversations are with people they already know, Farmers do not face much rejection. As a result, they do not require high levels of Emotional Toughness. Reasoning Ability can be important to Farmers, as the ability to diagnose and solve customer problems in a timely fashion creates the trust that forms the foundation of deep, long-term customer relationships. Service Drive is also important, but it must be tempered. Remember, a Farmer's goal should be to build and maintain *mutually* beneficial business relationships.

The *Hybrid* is capable of performing either the Hunter or Farmer role. These salespeople can be effective in securing new business *and* in deepening customer relationships, but it is very rare for both relationship preferences to be completely equal. Most Hybrid salespeople prefer one role to the other. The Hybrid salesperson who prefers the Hunter role is likely to have more churn in their account base and a higher rate of new account signups. The Hybrid salesperson who prefers the Farmer role will prospect effectively for a period of time. However, as soon as they have secured a sufficient number of accounts, they will happily focus their full attention on Farming these accounts.

Selling Styles

There are four primary selling styles:

1. **Consultative:** Consultative salespeople are very effective at asking questions, dissecting answers to identify possible needs, relating the needs to possible solutions, and planning additional questions. All of this is done on the fly while their prospect or customer is still talking. Consultative salespeople can be equally effective as Hunters, Farmers, or Hybrids.

2.   **Relationship:** Relationship salespeople build close, personal relationships with their prospects and customers. They win business by earning trust. They can be effective Hunters, but usually prefer to be Farmers.

3.   **Display:** Display salespeople work in department stores or other similar environments. The goods they sell are on display, and customers come to them. Their primary responsibilities are answering customers' questions and processing orders. From this standpoint their role is more similar to customer service than it is to the Hunter, Farmer, or Hybrid sales roles.

4.   **Hard Closer:** Hard Closers are what most people think of when they describe someone as "a used-car salesperson." These salespeople are very aggressive and don't readily take no for an answer. They are much more interested in making sales than they are in building relationships with customers. They are Hunters to the bone.

To develop a deeper understanding of these four selling styles, consider how the weightings differ for the four Critical Attributes for sales success. This information is summarized in Table 5.

Table 5: Sales Style and Critical Attributes

	Sales Drive	Emotional Toughness	Reasoning Ability	Service Drive
Consultative	High/ Medium	High/ Medium	High	High/ Medium/ Low
Relationship	High/ Medium	Medium/ Low	High/ Medium	High/ Medium
Display	Low	Low	Medium/ Low	High/ Medium
Hard Closer	High	High	Low	Low

If a *Consultative* salesperson is acting in a Hunter or Hybrid role, they need a stronger Sales Drive, more Emotional Toughness, and less Service Drive than they do if they are acting in a Farmer role. The one constant for Consultative salespeople is Reasoning Ability, as the basis of this selling style is the ability to ask excellent questions and rapidly abstract conclusions from the answers.

Relationship salespeople can also be effective as Hunters, Farmers, and Hybrids. Depending on the role, a strong Sales Drive may or may not be a requirement. Reasoning Ability is useful, but it is not as critical to Relationship salespeople as it is to Consultative salespeople. The required amount of Emotional Toughness will be determined by the type of sales role, the size of the salesperson's network of contacts, and the amount of prospecting they will be required to perform. Relationship salespeople do need healthy amounts of Service Drive, as this attribute compels them to pursue timely resolution to prospect and customer questions and issues. This in turn creates the foundation for trust, which is the basis of solid, long-term relationships.

Display salespeople are usually order takers with a customer-service focus. Some Display salespeople are quite aggressive and proactive; however, most Display salespeople are relatively passive. Their role requires neither a strong Sales Drive nor a high level of Emotional Toughness. They do need to have a reasonable amount of Reasoning Ability and Service Drive, as a key responsibility is responding effectively and accurately to customer questions and requests.

Hard Closers tend to have an overdeveloped Sales Drive, very high Emotional Toughness, a low Reasoning Ability, and a low Service Drive. They churn through a lot of prospects and receive enormous amounts of rejection. This style of selling tends to be most effective for selling relatively inexpensive products or services in markets that have an almost unlimited number of prospects. A large volume of prospects is a requirement, as Hard Closers usually burn bridges behind them.

CHAPTER 5

DEFINING YOUR COMPANY'S SALES JOB

The fifteen questions listed in this chapter do not identify every possible factor that a company should analyze when considering the desired attributes, personality preferences, and sales styles for their sales team members. However, the process of reviewing these questions usually sparks additional thoughts concerning desired salesperson attributes. At minimum, if a company develops carefully considered answers for these questions, it will be more consciously aware of the requirements for its sales position(s) than it was previously.

1. **Nature of the Customer:** What are your target markets? Are they horizontal or vertical? Do you sell to consumers, corporations, schools, state and local governments, etc.? What level(s) in the organization do you sell to? (Examples include purchasing, business unit manager, C-level executive, etc.)

Target markets drive numerous selling parameters, including the typical sales cycle length, prime selling seasons, and specific knowledge or experience that may be required to earn credibility with prospects and customers. Selling effectively to C-level executives (CEO, CFO, CIO, etc.) and other high-ranking officials definitely requires different attributes and skills than selling to purchasing agents.

2. **Nature of the Offering:** Is the offering complex or relatively simple? Is it tangible or intangible? Does it consist of a single product or service, or a combination of products and services? Does the company have a small portfolio of offerings or a large portfolio of offerings?

The nature of the offering(s) will impact key parameters, such as Sales Style, and the desirability of selected attributes, such as Reasoning Ability.

3. **Sales Environment:** What kind of environment do the salespeople work in? Are they office-based or home-based? Is most of their selling done over the phone or in person?

Salespeople who work from a home office typically require more strength in the attributes of Energy and Independence than office-based salespeople. Office-based salespeople can usually expect to receive more frequent direction and support from a sales manager.

4. **Geography:** How many sales locations does your company have? Where are they located?

Different sales approaches are often required to be successful in vastly different locales, such as downtown Manhattan, Baton Rouge, and Los Angeles.

5. **Sales Style:** Which sales style(s) are most effective in your target markets?

- Consultative
- Relationship
- Display
- Hard Closer

The nature of the customer and the complexity of the offering(s) should be considered when answering this question.

6. **Relationship Preference:** Is your company more interested in:

- Finding new customers (Hunter)
- Increasing account penetration and managing long-term relationships (Farmer)
- Both (Hybrid); if "Both," please list desired percentages for Hunter versus Farmer

Does your company wish to prioritize seeking new business or deepening account penetration? Or, is it important for your salespeople to accomplish some of both? As we learned in Chapter 4, it is rare for a salesperson to be completely ambivalent about Hunting versus Farming. Usually salespeople prefer one type of relationship to the other. If a company truly wants to accomplish both new business and account penetration sales goals, it should consider staffing separate Hunter and Farmer sales positions.

7. **Sales Cycle Length:** How often do salespeople have opportunities to present and persuade (close sales)? Several per day? Several per month? Several per year?

If a salesperson receives gratification from persuading and presenting, he or she won't be happy in a role that offers just a handful of opportunities per year to exercise these capabilities. A salesperson with a strong Sales Drive is better suited to selling offerings that have shorter sales cycles and higher volumes of opportunities. The converse is also true. A salesperson who lacks a strong Sales Drive may be better suited to longer, more complex sales cycles.

8. **Prospecting:** Do prospects come to the salesperson, or must the salesperson seek them out? If both scenarios apply, estimate a percentage for each.

If a sales position requires a lot of prospecting, the salesperson should have a strong Sales Drive, high Emotional Toughness (they *will* receive a lot of rejection), a positive Attitude, and high Energy.

9. **Administration:** Which job-related functions require attention to detail? Examples include making accurate forecasts, providing timely updates to the corporate CRM system, analyzing customer records to determine sales strategies, and ensuring regulatory compliance.

Some companies have support personnel who perform administrative tasks on their salespeople's behalf. Other companies expect their salespeople to deal with a certain amount of administration. If a tolerance for process, detail, and administration is necessary, some amount of Tolerance for Administration is desirable.

10. **Communication:** How important are verbal and written communication skills to sales success? Are the salespeople required to make presentations? Are they required to compose letters or proposals?

Roles that rely heavily on high-quality verbal and written communications require salespeople who have healthy amounts of Communication Skills and Reasoning Ability.

11. **Pre-sales Support:** What support resources are available to help salespeople manage specific steps of the sales cycle? How effective must the salesperson be at resource management?

The availability of support resources has a significant impact on the attributes required for sales success. For example, if salespeople have access to quality internal (employed by their company) or external (employed by suppliers or partners) technical resources, they don't need to invest a lot of time learning technical details. This frees them to focus more time and energy on prospecting and opportunity qualification. Also, if companies employ technical writers who can assist salespeople with large proposals and bid responses, there may be less need for the salespeople to have strong Communication Skills.

12. **Post-sales support:** Is the salesperson expected to provide technical or operational support to customers, or do other personnel provide this support?

If a salesperson is required to deliver post-sales support, it might be desirable for them to have a lower Sales Drive, be less Competitive, and have a higher Service Drive.

13. **Training:** What kinds of training does your company provide to salespeople? How much training does your company provide?

Companies that provide a lot of training may have the luxury of being able to hire inexperienced sales candidates and "train them up from scratch." This is extremely valuable in markets where highly qualified sales candidates are scarce and/or prohibitively expensive. However, if a company is going to follow this approach, it should seek candidates with strong Learning Rates.

14. **Sales Manager's Style:** What is the sales manager's style? Is the manager more of a Field General or an Administrator?

The desired levels of Sales Drive, Service Drive, Assertiveness, Competitiveness, Independence, and Tolerance for Administration will differ based upon the sales manager's style. See Chapter 7 for further explanation.

15. **Career Path:** What is the career path for the sales position? From small-ticket-item sales to

big-ticket-item sales? From sales to management?

If a company expects to use its sales team as a source of candidates for other positions, it should consider whether salespeople and sales candidates have the attributes required to be successful in the other positions. For example, most small-ticket-item sales cycles are shorter than big-ticket-item sales cycles. Per Question #7, the desired amount of Sales Drive will differ based upon the frequency of opportunities for presentation and persuasion. A successful salesperson in small-ticket-item sales will probably have a strong Sales Drive. Will that person become frustrated by the reduction in opportunities to present and persuade that could result from a "promotion" to big-ticket-item sales?

Similarly, the attributes required to be an effective manager are often quite different from the attributes required to be an effective salesperson. Success in management frequently requires more attention to detail and an interest in delegation and mentoring. These requirements impact the target ranges for the attributes Sales Drive, Service Drive, Assertiveness, Competitiveness, Independence, and Tolerance for Administration.

CHAPTER 6

RECRUITING MYTHS

How can we apply our knowledge of the attributes required for sales success to improve the proportion of top performers on a sales team? A good place to start is with an overhaul of a company's recruiting ads and job descriptions.

Many recruiting ads and job descriptions include "knockout factors" that actually screen out qualified sales candidates. Here are two examples:

- **Education:** A requirement for an undergraduate degree, a graduate degree, or a degree in a specialized field of study (e.g., engineering)

- **Experience:** A requirement for a minimum number of years of sales experience, or a minimum number of years experience selling a particular category of offering

It is easy to rationalize why education appears to be a reliable knockout factor. A manager might think, "We have a very technical offering. You really need to be an engineer to understand it. So, we should focus our recruiting efforts on individuals with engineering degrees." Or, an alternative line of thinking might be, "Our product line is constantly changing, and we have a rapid rate of new product introductions. Our salespeople need to be pretty sharp to keep up with all of the new product knowledge. So, we should only hire people with college degrees, as these people have proven they know how to learn."

These lines of thinking seem logical. However, are people with engineering degrees really the *only* ones who can understand detailed technical information? Also, how does the acquisition of a college degree identify whether an individual learns *quickly* or *slowly* (bucket versus milk jug)?

Another common mistake is focusing recruiting efforts on candidates who meet certain minimum requirements for amount or type of sales experience. This practice is based upon expectations that past sales experience will produce future sales results, and that these candidates will not require a lot of (sales skills and product knowledge) training. Their experience is expected to enable them to hit the ground running. As a result, companies are often willing to pay a premium to attract experienced candidates.

Unfortunately, there is compelling evidence that the vast majority of the time, hiring experienced sales candidates accomplishes nothing more than *the recycling of mediocrity*. If we revisit the statistics that were referenced in Chapter 2, fully 55 percent of salespeople should be doing something else for a living, and another 20 to 25 percent are selling the wrong type of offering. Based upon these statistics, the practice of hiring experienced sales candidates will produce an unsatisfactory result as much as 80 percent of the time!

A much better indicator of future success is whether a company's sales candidates have the attributes required for success in that company's specific sales job. Candidates who have the attributes required for sales success *and* significant experience selling similar offerings are truly ideal candidates. However, if a company has to choose between experienced candidates who lack key attributes required for sales success, and inexperienced candidates who have all of the attributes required for sales success, which candidates should the company choose? They should choose the inexperienced candidates! Why? A lack of experience can be overcome with training. A lack of the attributes required for sales success cannot!

Performance-Based Recruiting

To improve the overall quality of your sales candidate pool, shift your focus away from skills and experience and toward *performance-based measures*. For example, it is probably more important for sales candidates to have extensive and well-developed networks of business contacts than it is for them to have college degrees. Also, consider how you will measure a new salesperson's performance during their first thirty, sixty, ninety, and 180 days. What *activities* will you expect them to perform?

What *results* do you expect these activities to produce, and in what time frame? (See Chapter 14: Inspect Activities, Not Just Results.)

If you include performance-based language in your recruiting ads, you will start attracting fewer poor candidates, as some will self-select out. You will also start attracting more strong candidates, as they will no longer be screened out by invalid "knockout factors."

For more information on performance-based recruiting ads, performance-based interviewing, and other effective recruiting practices, see Lou Adler's book, *Hire With Your Head*. (See Appendix C: Suggested Reading.)

CHAPTER 7

THE IMPACT OF SALES MANAGER STYLE

How can a sales manager use the information provided in the preceding chapters to build a top-performing sales team? The first step is for the sales manager to understand how their own attributes and management style match up (or conflict) with the members of their sales team. To create a framework for this understanding, we will examine two sales management styles that are on the opposite ends of the spectrum: The Field General and The Administrator.

The Field General

Field Generals usually have a history of top sales performance. As salespeople, they were often the best of the best. No one sold more than they did, or took as much satisfaction from bringing in "the really tough deal." These managers have high levels of Sales Drive, Assertiveness, Competitiveness, Energy, and Independence.

Conversely, they tend to have relatively low levels of Service Drive and Tolerance for Administration. On average they tend to be Hunters rather than Farmers.

How do these attributes impact the Field General's management style? Field Generals are often in competition with their sales team. They don't want to spend their time coaching, nurturing, or supporting. They want to be in the spotlight! As a result, they are usually most effective when called in to help close a tough deal, or to help break down a roadblock that is delaying a sales cycle within their company.

Field Generals are usually not very good at administrative details and activities like sales reports, expense reports, activity inspection, coaching, mentoring, and helping salespeople plan go-to-market strategies. They would much rather be in the trenches than in the office.

What is the best type of sales team for a Field General? One made up of salespeople that share similar attributes. Field Generals work best with salespeople that are Assertive, Independent, somewhat organized, have high Energy, and require little direction. The only time the Field General is likely to hear from these salespeople is if they need help with a deal, and that is the way the Field General likes it.

The Administrator

The Administrator is the polar opposite of the Field General. Administrators do not always earn their management stripes through exemplary sales performance. The ones who do are usually Consultative or Relationship salespeople with a preference for Farming.

An Administrator is often seen as a "people person" who is expected to be a very hands-on manager. Administrators are selected due to their capabilities in the areas of delegation, planning, mentoring, coaching, team-building, and administration.

As you might expect, the attribute strengths of an Administrator are opposite those of a Field General. Administrators usually score higher in Service Drive and Tolerance for Administration, and lower in Sales Drive and Competitiveness. They can work effectively with salespeople who have a lower Sales Drive, are less Assertive, and are lower in Energy and Independence (i.e., externally motivated). These salespeople require frequent managerial direction and motivation in order to maximize sales performance.

The Importance of "Attribute Awareness"

Does this mean that every sales manager is either a Field General or an Administrator? Of course not! The Field General and Administrator examples are provided to demonstrate the opposite ends of the sales management style spectrum. Most sales managers fall somewhere in between these two style extremes. However, the Field General and Administrator examples help make the point that it is important for sales managers to understand their own attributes, and to know how their attributes complement or conflict with the attributes of each member of their sales team.

If a sales team consists of a mix of independent, self-motivated salespeople and highly manageable, externally motivated salespeople, the sales manager needs to make a choice. They can choose to minimize their interactions with the salespeople who have attributes that are uncomfortable for the sales manager to deal with, and look to replace these salespeople over time. Or, they can work individually with each salesperson to identify a level of interaction and support that is reasonably comfortable and productive for both parties.

CHAPTER 8

HOW TO DEVELOP AN EFFECTIVE PROSPECTING PLAN

Some companies do such a terrific job of demand generation (advertising, direct mail, telemarketing, etc.) that their salespeople never have to prospect. These lucky salespeople have access to more leads than they will ever have time to pursue. Unfortunately, the reality in most companies is that salespeople must source some or all of their own leads if they are to have any hope of achieving their sales targets. A comprehensive Prospecting Plan will help salespeople maximize their return on prospecting time invested.

What is a Prospecting Plan? Basically, it is a calendar that lists the various prospecting activities in which a salesperson plans to engage and the amount of time they intend to invest in each activity. The most effective prospecting plans don't focus on a single type of activity; rather, they include a mix of activities. A number of typical activities are examined below.

Cold-Calling

Cold-calling has probably dissuaded more people from pursuing a sales career than any other activity. After all, what could possibly be less fun than calling strangers, disrupting the flow of their busy day, and trying to convince them that they need to speak with you? When you receive a sales cold call, how does it make you feel? Do you enjoy the experience?

The basic challenge with cold-calling is that you are asking people for something (their time) before you have given them anything of value. Author and speaker Jeffrey Gitomer makes the case that cold-calling is a complete waste of time. He feels that salespeople can earn much greater returns by reallocating cold-calling time to networking and seeking referrals.

If you find that you *must* make cold calls, pick up a copy of Anthony Parinello's book, *Selling to VITO: The Very Important Top Officer* (see Appendix C: Suggested Reading). Parinello's comprehensive cold-calling methodology will teach you how to use *quantified business impacts* (see Chapter 9: The Secret to Closing More Sales) to stand out from other salespeople and attract the attention of C-level executives.

Networking

Many salespeople have a mistaken impression that networking is similar to cold-calling. When they attend networking events, they pass out business cards like candy and dive into sales pitches at every opportunity. When they make phone calls to the stacks of business cards they collect, they find they have no more success booking appointments than they do when making cold calls. What are they doing wrong?

These salespeople simply don't know how to network effectively. Effective networking requires getting to know people as *individuals* and learning what constitutes opportunities for *them*. Armed with this information, effective networkers become "matchmakers," matching contacts who have specific needs with other contacts who supply solutions to those needs. They do this with no expectation of personal benefit; however, the grateful people they help usually return the favor.

Networking can take a lot of forms. There are formal "leads clubs" that restrict their memberships to ensure that every member is in a different type of business. Each member is expected to bring leads for other members to every meeting (though in practice only a handful of leads club members seem to take this responsibility seriously). There are also networking events that are sponsored by any number of organizations, such as chambers of commerce, convention and visitor's bureaus, trade and professional associations, special interest groups, etc.

If you are considering including networking as an element of your prospecting plan (and you should!), here are three tips that will help you maximize your return on time invested:

1. **Get Some Training:** Learn how to network properly. Dave Sherman, "The Networking Guy," has published an excellent book entitled, *The Networking Guy's Top 50 Tips: A Simple Guide to Networking Success*. He sells this book,

instructional tapes, and CDs on his website: www.thenetworkingguy.com.

2. **Bring Unusual "Handouts":** What unusual items can you bring to networking events that will attract the attention of other attendees? My personal choice is fifteen copies of a glossy, laminated, full-color piece that looks like the front and back covers of this book. Definitions for the twelve attributes required for sales success are printed on the inside, along with my contact information. People often sneak covert glances at these pieces, providing a natural entrée for conversations.

3. **Look for Unusual Ways to Network:** Consider becoming an "ambassador" with your local chamber of commerce. Ambassadors help staff events, conduct initiation meetings with new members, and conduct fact-finding meetings (to solicit suggestions for improving chamber programs and services) with experienced members. These types of activities can provide opportunities to build relationships with numerous potential prospects. Also consider doing volunteer work with charitable organizations. Keep an eye out for opportunities that provide exposure to the organization's board of directors. Board members are often well connected in the community, which makes them excellent potential referral sources.

Referrals

A referral is an introduction to a potential prospect that is made by someone the prospect knows and respects. It is important to recognize that all referrals are not created equal. Here are several categories of referrals, ranging from most effective to least effective:

1. **Live, In-Person Introduction:** This is when your contact walks you over to a potential prospect and makes an introduction. In an ideal circumstance, the introduction includes a glowing testimonial about you, your offering, and/or your company.

2. **Live Telephone Introduction:** If time or circumstances do not permit a live, in-person introduction (for example, your contact and the prospect work in different facilities), the next-best option is a live telephone introduction. This might take the form of a conference call or a call from a speakerphone in your contact's office. Your contact may participate in the entire conversation with the prospect, or they may drop out of the call after making the introductions.

3. **Electronic Introduction:** If you cannot arrange for a live, in-person or telephone introduction, the next best option is for your contact to speak with, leave a voice mail for, or send an e-mail to the prospect prior to you contacting them. When you make your introductory call, be sure to mention that "(Name)

recently contacted you to introduce me and explain why he/she thinks it is a good idea for us to get together.

4. **Authorized Name Dropping:** The lowest level of referral is when your contact gives you a prospect's name and phone number and permission to mention their name when you call the prospect. This is "warmer" than a cold call, but it is not as effective as other types of referrals.

How do you earn referrals? The absolute best way is by providing *great* service to your customers. It is also helpful if you set an expectation that referrals are your preferred reward for providing exceptional service.

When should you ask for referrals? Every time there is an opportunity to do so! When you do a favor for a customer, ask for referrals. When a customer places an order, ask for referrals. If a customer comments that they are happy with something that you or your company did, ask for referrals. When you help a customer solve a problem, ask for referrals.

Customers are not the only source for referrals. Anyone you interact with while conducting Prospecting Plan activities is a potential source of referrals. If you feel you have built credibility with someone, or they seem interested in what you do, do not hesitate to ask them for referrals.

Strategic Alliances

No matter what kinds of offerings you sell, there are companies that provide *complementary* products and services. If you create strategic alliances with these companies, you will be introduced to opportunities that you might not otherwise have found.

80/20 Performance, Inc. helps companies identify the attributes required for success in particular sales roles. One of the ways we use this information is to identify individualized training needs for existing sales team members. However, we do not provide training services. When we identify a training need, we refer our customer to a strategic partner that specializes in the appropriate type of training. Likewise, when our strategic partners' customers need help beating the 80/20 rule in selling, our partners refer them to us.

You might also explore strategic alliances where your offering becomes one component of a larger, more comprehensive offering. In this scenario, whenever you or your strategic partner sells the combined offering, both of you win business.

It is possible to manage multiple strategic alliances, but this works best if your strategic partners do not compete directly with each other. Also, it is important to recognize that strategic alliances only bear fruit when the participants are *serious* about the relationship. This means that alliance partners must be willing to dedicate time and resources to finding opportunities for each other. Finally, it is critical that you follow through on any and all commitments that you make to your alliance partners and their customers. Your strategic partners are putting their own credibility and reputations on the line when they refer their customers to you. Don't let them down!

Speaking

Speaking enables you to deliver your message to multiple potential prospects at once. A well-constructed speech, seminar, or webinar (online seminar) can increase your credibility with prospects and establish you as an expert in your field. Plus, every speech has the potential to reach far beyond the original audience. If you deliver a compelling message, there is no telling how many times it will be repeated to others by your audience members.

What should you speak about? Look for topics that are of particular interest to your target prospects. Offer new approaches for solving especially troubling business problems. Educate your prospects on compelling new technologies or other concepts that will help them professionally or personally. Discuss real-life case studies and share stories. Engage your audience by conducting polls and giving them opportunities to ask questions and provide feedback.

Be very careful about selling from the podium. Audiences become disenchanted very quickly when they feel a speech is nothing more than a thinly disguised sales pitch. However, it *is* perfectly appropriate to include a gentle call to action at the end of your speech. Consider closing with a statement such as, "If you would like to explore the possibility of applying the concepts that were discussed during today's presentation to *your* company, please give me your business card or call me at your convenience." Many times interested prospects will approach you with questions following the conclusion of your speech.

Preparing for seminars and speeches is a lot of work. You need to prepare your presentation materials, write scripts, and practice them to the point where you can deliver your presentation smoothly and convincingly. You also need to secure a facility for your speech and make arrangements for any necessary audio/visual equipment. If you are going to serve refreshments, there are additional arrangements to make. Plus, you need to develop and implement a plan for attracting an audience. This might include sending direct mail or e-mails, making phone calls, and contacting trade, professional, and social associations and organizations.

If you are going to invest the time and effort required to deliver a first-class event, you should also develop a plan for maximizing the return on your investment. Be sure to give your audience a form they can use to request additional information. Provide handouts that include presentation highlights and your contact information. Hold a drawing for some type of small prize (a book, a sample product, etc.) to encourage attendees to give you business cards. Block some time during the day or two following your presentation to make phone calls to audience members. Ask them for feedback, and give them opportunities to ask questions that might not have been answered during the event. Also ask for referrals to people they know who might be interested in your presentation topic. These referrals may become immediate prospects; at minimum they should be added to your invitation list for future events.

Writing

If you have a talent for writing, you can use it to help you build credibility and relationships with suspects, prospects, and customers. Write articles and submit them to your local business journal or newspaper. Submit articles to trade publications and any other publications that your prospects might read. Write and publish a monthly newsletter that includes articles on topics that are of particular interest to your target prospects. Contribute articles to newsletters that are published by strategic partners, chambers of commerce, or local networking organizations. When any of your articles are published, acquire paper or electronic copies and share them with suspects, prospects, and customers.

Creating the Best Plan for YOU

How can you devise the Prospecting Plan that will be most effective for *you*? Begin by identifying your best prospects. The questions listed in Chapter 5: Defining Your Sales Job will help you accomplish this task. Once you have identified target prospects, find out where and how they cluster. Do they belong to specific trade, professional, or social associations or organizations? Do they attend specific networking events? Do they serve on boards of directors for certain charities? If you are not sure, ask some of your customers. They will be happy to share this information with you.

Next, decide which types of prospecting activities will provide the best opportunities to interact with your target prospects. Also, try to choose activities that match your talents and interests. If you *enjoy* your prospecting activities, you will perform them more frequently and effectively. If your prospecting plan includes some activities that you don't really enjoy, be especially disciplined in how you schedule and perform these activities. Seek training in proven methodologies to improve your effectiveness.

Don't be afraid to exercise some creativity in your prospecting activities. For example, if you don't enjoy cold-calling for appointments, try cold-calling to fill seats for a seminar. Look for low-key ways to interact with your target prospects and get to know them as people. The impact on your opportunity pipeline will be both significant and gratifying.

CHAPTER 9

THE SECRET TO CLOSING MORE SALES

Many sales methodology training courses focus considerable attention on closing techniques. In fact, there are entire books written about how to close sales. Certainly closing is an important activity, as the time, effort, and resources invested in managing sales cycles are wasted if orders are not secured. However, the real secret to closing sales is doing a great job at the *front* end of the sales cycle. In other words, it is the quality of the work that is done during the *opportunity qualification* stage of the sales process that determines whether a sale will close, as well as how hard or easy it will be to close. Doing a great job of opportunity qualification also minimizes the amount of time, energy, and resources that are wasted on opportunities that will never close, or that will produce only marginally profitable or unprofitable business.

At its simplest, opportunity qualification is the process of determining whether a prospect has enough interest in a product, service, or solution for them to justify engaging in a sales cycle. At its most effective, opportunity qualification is *a two-way street*. What does this mean? It means you shouldn't focus solely on whether a prospect can be enticed into a sales cycle. You should also carefully consider whether the prospect is worthy of the time and resource investments that will be required to manage a sales cycle. The best way to accomplish this level of qualification is to break the process into three separate steps: Business Problem Qualification, M-A-I-N BP Qualification, and Technical/Detailed Qualification. Each of these steps is explained below.

Business Problem Qualification

Business Problem Qualification is the process of asking questions to determine whether a prospect has any of the *business problems* that your company's offerings can address, and to *quantify the impact* of these business problems.

What is a business problem? A business problem is any activity or outcome that negatively impacts a business. Examples of negative impacts include reductions in revenue, profits, customer satisfaction, employee productivity, job satisfaction, etc. Here is an example of a business problem description:

Many mission-critical software applications (e-business, manufacturing, point-of-sale, etc.) need to access relational databases in order to function. If a database has problems (goes down or suffers data loss or corruption), application downtime can cost companies tens of thou-

sands of dollars per minute in lost sales, lost customers, and lost opportunities.

Unfortunately, most product/service/solution sales training programs do not address business problems. Instead, they focus on teaching salespeople to regurgitate exhaustive lists of product *features* and *benefits*. There is some value in a salesperson being aware of key features and benefits, as features are what provide solutions to business problems. However, if salespeople just spew long lists of features and benefits at prospects, in essence they are hoping that the prospects are already aware of their own business problems, and will somehow figure out for themselves which features can solve their business problems. This is a very inefficient way to sell. Plus, salespeople run the risk that prospects will *not* figure out the linkages between business problems and features, or that prospects will become bored and switch off before potentially valuable features are identified.

Business problem identification is too important to leave to chance. Salespeople sell much more effectively and efficiently when they become conversant in the specific business problems that each of their offerings address, and the questions they can ask to determine whether these business problems exist. This type of training is discussed in Chapter 15: Why Most Sales Training Programs Fail.

Even when salespeople become experts in business problems and qualifying questions, their education is not complete. Salespeople also need to be taught questions they can ask to *quantify the impact* of specific business problems. Quantified impacts are *dollar values* or *percentages* with associated *time frames* that can be assigned to specific business problems. For example, in the earlier business problem description, the quantified impact is "tens of thousands of dollars per minute."

Quantified impacts are an invaluable aid to closing sales. How? If the quantified impact of a business problem exceeds the investment required to fix the problem, a buying decision becomes easy to justify. The larger the difference is between the quantified impact and the required investment, the easier it becomes to close the sale. If the quantified impact is a multiple of the required investment (for example, a quantified impact of *millions* of dollars versus a required investment of *thousands* of dollars), the buying decision becomes a no-brainer.

Here is an important caveat: In order for a quantified impact to add value to the selling process, the *prospect* must be the source of the numbers. Why? In general, prospects don't trust salespeople. Many have been exposed to Hunters/Hard Closers who were more interested in making sales than they were in providing value. Plus, prospects recognize that salespeople have a vested interest in building a compelling business case that can be used to support a buying decision. This causes prospects to discount any information that salespeople provide. However, if the *prospect* is the source of the information, it takes on the veneer of unquestioned truth. This makes learning how to ask *quantifying* questions a valuable skill indeed!

M-A-I-N BP Qualification

Many salespeople are desperate to engage prospects in sales cycles. After all, it is much more fun to manage sales cycles than it is to prospect. Plus, they get to add opportunities to their pipeline, which gives their sales manager the impression that they are actually doing something useful. These salespeople have blind faith that if they can somehow convince prospects to engage in sales cycles, they will eventually make sales. This belief causes them to indiscriminately invest time, effort, and company resources in any prospect that expresses even the slightest interest in one of their offerings.

Unfortunately, sales cycle time and resource investments do not inevitably produce sales. How many of the opportunities in your pipeline have been stalled at the same step in the sales cycle for weeks...or months? In how many opportunities has your company invested enormous amounts of time, energy, and resources (conducting product demonstrations, writing lengthy proposals, facilitating product evaluations, etc.), only to have the prospect either choose not to buy or prove incapable of securing necessary financing? Even when sales are made, how many turn out to be nightmare customers who are always dissatisfied and consume huge amounts of post-sales resources?

All prospects are *not* created equal. Salespeople do need to help prospects explore whether their business problems are substantial enough to justify investing time in a sales cycle (Business Problem Qualification). However, salespeople *also* need to determine whether the prospect is worthy of time and resource investments by the salesperson's company. If a prospect is not a good fit, a wise salesperson disengages from the opportunity (why not refer them to a competitor and let the competitor burn some cycles?) and searches for other prospects.

How can salespeople accomplish this type of qualification? Many sales methodology training courses teach an acronym, M-A-N, that stands for **M**oney, **A**uthority, and **N**eed. The idea is to determine whether: (1) the prospect is willing to commit enough budget dollars (Money) to pay for the offering; (2) the key decision-makers and influencers (Authority) have been identified; and (3) the prospect's pain (Need) is severe enough to justify investing in a solution.

Unfortunately, even when salespeople do a good job of M-A-N qualification, they can be blindsided by issues that delay sales cycles or destroy opportunities outright. For example, some prospects prove incapable of securing the financing necessary to fund their budgets. (In other words, they are not credit worthy.) Some decision-makers need to have specific information provided in a specific format before they can authorize a buying decision. Sometimes salespeople invest considerable time and effort in troubleshooting complex problems and designing solutions, only to be informed that the prospect must take the proposed solution out to bid. This can lead to the opportunity being lost to a low bidder or the profitability of the opportunity being decimated.

To avoid these issues, salespeople should add additional questions to the M-A-N qualification process. The acronym that I have assigned to this revised process is M-A-I-N BP, which stands for **M**oney, **A**uthority,

Information, **N**eed, and **B**uying **P**rocess. A sample M-A-I-N BP qualification form is provided in Appendix A.

When salespeople successfully complete both Business Problem Qualification and M-A-I-N BP Qualification, management is able to make very educated resource allocation decisions. Expensive time and resources can be laser-focused on opportunities that have the best chance of producing attractive returns on investment.

Business Problem and M-A-I-N BP qualification should *not* be one-time activities, especially if sales cycles extend over weeks or months. It is entirely possible for decision-makers to change, business priorities to change, budget allocations to change, etc. The most successful salespeople periodically *revisit* opportunity qualification to ensure that no substantial changes that might delay or derail the sales cycle have occurred.

Technical/Detailed Qualification

Technical/Detailed Qualification takes place after Business Problem and M-A-I-N BP qualification have been completed, and after *a conscious decision* has been made to invest time and resources in pursuing a sales cycle. In Technical/Detailed Qualification, the selling company's technical (and other) experts work with the prospect company's experts to troubleshoot business problems, determine root causes, and identify potential solutions.

If the selling company's salespeople have extensive technical knowledge, they may be directly involved in some or all of these activities. However, a better use of most salespeople's time is to assume the role of "resource manager" and leverage the expertise of others. In this model, salespeople are not required to become experts in the intricacies of their offerings. Instead, they become experts in *finding and qualifying opportunities* and *leveraging expert resources* to help them convert opportunities into sales. This approach reduces the time required for new salespeople to become effective prospectors, and accelerates traction by all salespeople when new offerings are introduced. For more information on this approach to selling, see Chapter 15: Why Most Sales Training Programs Fail.

Closing

If salespeople do a superior job of qualifying opportunities, closing sales becomes simple and matter-of-fact. I have been a student of consultative selling for sixteen-plus years, and I have used a grand total of four "closes" during my career. These are the Financial Close, the Chronology Close, the Ben Franklin Close, and the Thermometer Close. Here are brief descriptions of these four closes:

1. **Financial Close:** A financial close is the natural choice when you have successfully helped your prospect quantify the impact of a business problem. As stated earlier, if the quantified impact of a business problem exceeds the investment required to solve it, a buying decision is simple to justify. The larger the difference is between the quantified impact and the required investment, the easier it becomes to close the sale.

2. **Chronology Close:** The chronology close is effective when an offering will impact a prospect's project plan, especially if the purchasing decision is a prerequisite to other activities in the project plan. If you start with the desired project completion date, then backtrack through project milestones to the point where your company's offering should be added, in many cases you and your prospect will discover that an order should have already been placed!

3. **Ben Franklin Close:** Some prospects have a hard time making a buying decision, regardless of the potency of the business case that supports the decision. This is simply a reflection of their personality and behavioral traits. For these people, the Ben Franklin Close can be very effective.

The traditional delivery for the Ben Franklin Close begins with the salesperson reciting trite phrases such as, "Ben Franklin was considered by many to be a very wise man. Whenever he needed to make an important decision, he would..." If you wish, you can skip that part and get right to the core of the technique. Draw a vertical line down the middle of a sheet of paper, and a horizontal line that intersects the top of the vertical line. This creates a large "T" on the paper. On the left side of the "T," write the word "For." On the right side of the "T," write the word "Against."

Now, suggest to the prospect that it might be helpful to make a list of all of the reasons both for and against acquiring your offering. Help them create the longest possible list of entries in the "For" column. Let them populate the "Against" column by themselves. The usual end result is a list of reasons in the "For" column that is much longer than the list of reasons in the "Against" column. Seeing this difference visually can help push a reluctant prospect over the decision-making hump.

4.   **Thermometer Close:** In this close, the salesperson asks the prospect to rate their level of interest on a zero-to-ten scale. Zero means the prospect has no interest at all, and ten means they have already decided to buy. If the prospect answers "Ten," you're done. Stop talking and write up the order. If the prospect's answer is a five or lower, ask, "Based upon what you've told me so far, I don't understand why you say (score). Can you help me understand that?" Their answer will tell you what you need to do to advance the sales cycle. If the prospect's answer is a six or more, ask them, "What do you need to see to get to ten?" Again, their answer will tell you what you need to do.

One of the attractions of this close is that it can be used repeatedly. As the prospect's "temperature" rises, you can continue to ask them, "What do you need to see to get to ten?" This is a nice, nonthreatening way to get the prospect to share with you any issues that are separating you from a sale.

The Value of Testimonials

Another tremendous sales-closing aid is customer testimonials. What is a testimonial? It is a written statement from an existing customer that explains how you, your offering, and/or your company delivered value to that customer's business. These statements may be as brief as a single sentence, or they may be as lengthy as a multi-page case study.

Testimonials may be general statements of satisfaction, or they may be very explicit, step-by-step descriptions of how value was provided. The best testimonials include quantified business impacts (i.e., dollar values or percentages and time frames). Note that there is a difference between a quantified impact that is developed during Business Problem Qualification and a quantified impact that is documented in a Testimonial. The "Qualification" impact is a forecast or an estimate of *expected* results, while the "Testimonial" impact consists of *actual* results that have been delivered to the customer.

Helping customers calculate and document quantified business impacts has value beyond possible use in testimonials. This practice can also help you *keep* customers. How? Remember, circumstances change. Businesses see upturns and downturns in revenues and profits. Companies can be acquired by other companies, which can lead to significant changes in management teams. Individuals get promoted, leave companies to pursue other opportunities, and have health problems. All of these circumstances can impact *whether* your customers continue buying from you, and *how much* they buy from you.

What would happen to your sales volume if a key customer's business got "soft," or if their company was acquired by another company, or if your most vocal champion was reassigned or left to pursue another opportunity? If you have not helped this customer document quantified business impacts, the result may be a sudden drop in your sales. Why? Because the first things that get cut during business downturns or management changes are *those things that management does not understand.*

If your customers have thorough documentation on hand that clearly explains the quantified business impact of your offerings, the risk of a sudden drop in your sales volume is dramatically reduced. If there are any "why are we buying this" questions, you can review the quantified-business-impact documents with them. Once they see how your offerings generate value, they will usually focus their cost-cutting attention elsewhere.

How does a salesperson acquire testimonials? They *ask* for them! Just like with referrals, the best time to ask for testimonials is when customers are feeling happy and satisfied. If a customer makes a positive statement that you feel would make a good testimonial, ask them if they would be willing to put their thoughts into writing. If they hesitate because of the amount of time it would take, volunteer to write the testimonial for them. Put their key statements into an electronic document and send it to the customer. Upon receipt, all they will need to do is edit the document, print it on their company's letterhead, sign it, and deliver it back to you. If your customer is truly satisfied, they will be willing to invest this minimal amount of effort on your behalf.

While salespeople should make every effort to secure testimonials from their own customers, they can also benefit by leveraging testimonials that have been secured by other salespeople. Companies can facilitate this practice by investing the time and resources required to build a *centralized testimonial repository*. The testimonials contained in this repository should be coded to enable rapid sorting by industry, business problem, offering, etc. This makes it easy for salespeople to quickly find testimonials that are pertinent to specific prospect circumstances. It is also useful to document whether customers are willing to speak to potential prospects. If the answer is yes, any requests for such conversations should be routed through the salesperson who owns the customer relationship.

The quality of a centralized testimonial repository will be in direct correlation to the amount of effort and resources that a company invests in creating and maintaining it. If a company wants to make testimonial selling a key pillar of its sales culture, management should consider creating a "SWAT team" to help salespeople and customers identify and document quantified business impacts. Plus, one or more individuals could be assigned the responsibility of occasionally purging "aged" testimonials. (Ideally, all of the testimonials in the repository should be less than two years old.) Finally, companies should take steps to ensure that testimonials are still valid. In other words, they should ensure that customer-satisfaction phone calls or written surveys are completed on a regular (quarterly or semi-annual) basis.

This will minimize the chances of salespeople being embarrassed by using testimonials from companies that are presently unhappy or are no longer customers.

CHAPTER 10

FORECASTING AND PIPELINE MANAGEMENT

Companies base very important decisions on their sales-opportunity pipelines. Examples include employee headcount, inventory levels, marketing investments, etc. If opportunity pipelines are inaccurate, or if opportunities do not close in predictable time frames, it can wreak havoc on vital financial measurements such as revenue, profit, and cash flow. This makes maximizing the accuracy of sales forecasts and opportunity pipelines critical to every company's success.

What is the condition of your company's opportunity pipeline? How many opportunities are listed? What is the total dollar value of these opportunities? How many have been stalled at the same step in the sales cycle for extended periods (weeks or months)? Are your company's salespeople held accountable for producing accurate forecasts and maintaining current, accurate opportunity pipelines?

Opportunity Pipeline Report Data Elements

Including the following data elements will maximize the utility of opportunity pipeline reports for both salespeople and management:

1. **Salesperson Name:** This should be at the report header level for individual salesperson reports, and at the line item level for sales branch or company reports.

2. **Company Name:** This is the name of the prospect or customer company.

3. **Project Name:** Large and/or active accounts may have multiple opportunities in process at any point in time. Project Names can be used to distinguish multiple opportunities from each other. Additionally, Project Names can be used to aggregate opportunities that consist of multiple line items.

4. **Category (Optional):** Some constituencies within a company may wish to look at specific subsets of the opportunity pipeline. For example, marketing teams in an information technology company may wish to separately examine opportunities for hardware, software, services, etc.

5. **Subcategory (Optional):** A company may also wish to subdivide specific Categories. For example, the Category "Hardware" could be subdivided into subcategories such as Servers, Storage, Networking, etc.

6. **Revenue:** This is the gross revenue that an opportunity line item is expected to produce.

7. **Gross Margin Percentage (Optional):** If a company does not work from a fixed pricing schedule, it may wish to track the profitability of individual opportunity line items.

8. **Gross Margin (Optional):** If a company chooses to track the profitability of individual opportunity line items, it should calculate each line item's gross margin contribution by multiplying Revenue by Gross Margin Percentage.

9. **Book Month:** This is the month in which the sale is expected to close.

10. **Ship Month (Optional):** Sometimes booked orders can take weeks or months to ship (for example, if a product is on backorder). When this occurs, a company may wish to track both a Book Month and a Ship Month. This becomes especially pertinent if either revenue recognition or commissions are triggered by order shipment.

11. **Confidence Percentage:** This value identifies the likelihood of closing an order for the opportunity line item. For more information, see "Assigning Confidence Percentages to Opportunities" later in this chapter.

12. **Next Action Item:** This should be a text field where the salesperson can enter a brief

description of the next planned activity that will advance the opportunity toward closure.

13. **Owner:** This is the person or people who are responsible for completing the Next Action Item.

14. **Due Date:** This is the date when the Next Action Item is expected to be completed.

15. **Status:** This value identifies whether the opportunity line item has been Booked, Lost, or is still in process (Open).

Opportunity pipeline reports should be sorted first by Book Month or Ship Month, then by Status (showing Closed opportunity line items first, then Open line items; Lost line items should be listed last or on a separate report), then by Confidence Percentage, then by either Revenue or Gross Margin. When reports are sorted in this manner, report users can see at a glance (1) how much business has already been closed for the month; (2) the Open opportunities sequenced from those closest to closing to those furthest from closing; and (3) within each Confidence Percentage, the opportunities sequenced from largest to smallest in terms of Revenue or Gross Margin contribution.

Note to Management: If you want your salespeople to do a good job of updating opportunity records, there has to be something in it for them. One company I worked with couldn't understand why their salespeople did such a poor job of updating opportunity records. Upon further questioning, I learned that the company did not make *individual* opportunity pipeline reports available to its salespeople! Since the salespeople did not benefit from performing opportunity updates, they considered the task to be a low priority. When the company made individual reports available to its salespeople, pipeline accuracy and the timeliness of updates improved dramatically.

Using the Opportunity Pipeline Report

When I was a salesperson, my monthly commissions were based upon order shipments. As a result, my daily Opportunity Pipeline analysis always began with a quick review of Booked orders, with the question in mind, "Is there anything that I can do *today* that will help one of my Booked orders ship sooner?" Then I would look at each Open opportunity line item to review the Next Action Item, Owner, and Due Date. Regardless of whether the action item belonged to me, I would consider whether there was anything that *I* could do *that day* to push the opportunity closer to closure. If the action item was owned by a prospect or customer, I would consider whether there was any way that I could take the action item off their desk. After all, they had many other priorities, but *my* priority was accelerating sales cycles!

Once I had made a list of the pipeline-related tasks that I needed to perform that day, I would determine whether each task warranted the use of "selling time" (from 9 a.m. to 4 p.m.), or whether it could be performed during non-selling hours. When I completed all of my "during selling time" tasks, I would spend the rest of selling time prospecting for new opportunities.

I found this approach to be extremely effective. Daily attention applied to each opportunity helped me push sales cycles along at the fastest possible rate. Some days all of my selling time was consumed by activities that advanced existing opportunities. Other days it was spent solely on prospecting activities. Most days fell somewhere in between.

As a sales manager, I reviewed my sales branch's opportunity pipeline report with many of the same thoughts in mind. The major change was the handling of Next Action Items. On the day of or day following a Next Action Item Due Date, I would touch base with the appropriate salesperson to learn whether the Next Action Item had been completed as anticipated. If the answer was no, then I would ask the salesperson to update the Due Date. If the answer was yes, I would ask the salesperson to update the Next Action Item, Owner, and Due Date. I was very diligent with this inspection, and it trained my salespeople to pay close attention to Next Action Items and Due Dates. This discipline helped our entire sales team accelerate every sales cycle to the maximum extent possible.

Assigning Confidence Percentages to Opportunities

Confidence percentages should indicate how close an opportunity line item is to closing. This concept is not new to most salespeople and managers. The challenge is ensuring that the confidence percentages that are associated with individual opportunity line items are truly valid. This is best accomplished by publishing explicit definitions for confidence percentages and teaching salespeople to apply them correctly. Managers can help ingrain this behavior by conducting frequent "Pipeline Reviews" with their salespeople.

The number of percentages that companies choose to define should be based upon the answers to two key questions: (1) How many steps are there in a typical sales cycle? (2) How significant is each step in advancing the opportunity toward closure? There is little value in including percentages for every step in the sales cycle if the completion of specific steps does not measurably move the opportunity closer to closure.

Here are some sample percentages and related definitions. You may choose to add or remove percentages, or change the definitions that are assigned to specific percentages.

1. **10%:** Unqualified opportunity. This percentage is included to enable salespeople to track unqualified prospects; plus, it provides a useful measure of new prospecting activity.

2. **20%:** Business Problem Qualification completed (see Chapter 9)

3. **30%:** M-A-I-N BP Qualification completed (see Chapter 9)

4. **40%:** Quote or proposal submitted

5. **50%:** Competitor involved; 50/50 chance of winning

6. **60%:** Competitor involved; prospect/customer is leaning toward your company's solution

7. **80%:** Verbal commitment received from prospect/customer

8.   90%: Order booked

9.   100%: Order shipped

If you want to maximize the accuracy of your company's opportunity pipeline, pay special attention to the steps "Business Problem Qualification" and "M-A-I-N BP Qualification." When you start inspecting these two activities, you will be astonished to learn how many opportunities with high confidence percentages *have never been properly qualified!* It is no wonder that opportunities languish for weeks and months with no change in opportunity status.

Here is another suggestion. Don't allow salespeople to assign a Revenue value to an opportunity line item unless the Business Problem and M-A-I-N BP qualification steps have been completed *and* a quote or proposal has been submitted to the prospect or customer. This removes unqualified opportunities from pipeline dollar totals and improves the accuracy of dollar estimates for qualified opportunities. Implementing this discipline will dramatically improve the quality of your pipeline-based strategic decision making.

CHAPTER 11

HOW TO ASSIGN SALES TERRITORIES

As companies prepare to hire salespeople, they need to make decisions about Sales Territories. Sales territories are usually established for two primary purposes: (1) to foster penetration of a defined market, and (2) to prevent wasted resources, i.e., multiple salespeople investing time, effort, and company resources in pursuing the same accounts.

There are an infinite number of ways to define sales territories. Several of the most common are listed below.

- **Geography:** This includes defining territories by country, region, state, county, city, zip code, etc.

- **Vertical Market:** Examples of vertical markets include Manufacturing, Health Care, Financial Services, etc. Large vertical markets such as Manufacturing may be divided

into submarkets such as Discrete Manufacturing, Process Manufacturing, etc.

- **Named Account:** Accounts are assigned by
company name. Large accounts may be further subdivided by geography, division,
business unit, etc.

Most companies do not have enough salespeople
to accomplish any significant geographic market penetration. Besides, the most effective way for most salespeople to prospect is by asking for referrals (see Chapter
8: How to Develop a Prospecting Plan). Since referrals
can cross geographies and vertical markets, the most
effective means of territory assignment for most companies is by Named Account.

In the Named Account model, the decision as to
whether or not a salesperson is given ownership of an
account is usually determined by the size of the account,
the number of divisions, the depth to which the salesperson has penetrated the account, the level (titles) of
specific individuals with whom the salesperson has relationships, and whether any other salespeople have relationships in the account that can be leveraged to good
effect. If assignment of the account to one salesperson is
not clearly warranted, management has a number of
options they can consider. These include (1) assigning
multiple salespeople to separate divisions or business
units; (2) declaring a "jump ball," where salespeople
compete for the account's business; and (3) creating a
team approach where prospecting activities, sales, and
compensation are shared by two or more salespeople.

CHAPTER 12

HOW TO DEVELOP AN EFFECTIVE COMPENSATION PLAN

Many companies make the mistake of offering a 100-percent commission compensation plan. Why? This type of plan minimizes the company's risk, as no sales made means no commissions paid. Besides, any salesperson who is any good should have enough faith in their own ability to work on 100-percent commission, right?

It doesn't work that way. Any salesperson who *is* any good knows that it takes time to build an opportunity pipeline, regardless of how much experience they have or how robust their personal network is. They also know they will need to invest considerable time and effort in learning about their new employer and its offerings. They still need to pay their bills while this learning and pipeline building takes place. Not surprisingly, these talented salespeople usually choose to work for employers who are willing to make investments in them.

If you run an ad for a 100-percent commission sales job, what kinds of candidates can you expect to see? Usually they will fall into three categories:

1. **Manufacturers' Representatives:** These salespeople work as independent contractors, not employees. Usually they sell a portfolio of offerings on behalf of multiple client companies. Make no mistake—these are mercenary salespeople. The amount of time and effort they will invest in selling your company's offerings will correlate directly with the amount of return they feel they can earn on their investment. If other client companies offer more lucrative compensation plans, offer a monthly retainer, and/or do a better job of providing leads, don't expect to see much activity with your company's offerings.

2. **Newbies:** These candidates are exploring sales as a career for the first time. Because of their lack of experience, they may have difficulty finding jobs that aren't 100-percent commission; or, they may just not know any better. They may or may not have the attributes required for success in your particular sales job (80 percent of them won't), and they probably don't have the first clue about how to build an opportunity pipeline. Still, they may be willing to come on board and grind away for a few weeks. However, if they don't luck into some early sales, chances are excellent that they will drift away and look for an

employer who is willing to teach them how to sell *and* pay them something while they are learning.

3. **The "Other 80 Percent":** It is rare for a salesperson with talent and experience to consider a 100-percent commission sales job. If one does, it is even rarer for them to be one of the 20 percent of salespeople who produce 80 person of sales. Usually it will be someone from the 80 percent of salespeople who produce 20 percent of sales. Perhaps they are making a last-ditch effort before giving up on sales. Perhaps they need to be able to say they are employed while they search for another job. At any rate, the chances are poor that one of these salespeople will ever deliver more than mediocre performance.

Another challenge unique to 100-percent commission compensation plans is that the employer loses the ability to hold salespeople accountable for administrative activities. These activities include attending training sessions and meetings, working from the office on specific days, or updating the opportunity pipeline in a timely fashion. If a salesperson doesn't do what the employer asks, so what? What have they got to lose?

Providing an Income Floor

Compensation plans that attract and motivate quality salespeople usually include some type of *Income Floor*. This is a guaranteed minimum amount of compensation that the salesperson earns within a specified time period. The Income Floor is usually provided in one of three ways: via a Salary, a Recoverable Draw, or a Non-recoverable Draw. Here are definitions for these three terms:

1. **Salary:** This is a fixed amount of money that is paid within a specified time period. Any commissions earned (if applicable) are paid in addition to the salary.

2. **Recoverable Draw:** This is a fixed amount of money that is paid within a specified time period. However, think of it as commissions paid in advance. If the actual commissions earned during the time period exceed the draw amount, the salesperson is paid the difference at some later date. However, if the actual commissions earned during the time period do not equal or exceed the draw amount, the salesperson owes the company the difference. Any commissions in excess of draw that are earned in future time periods will first be applied to liquidate any negative balance in the salesperson's draw account before commission payments are made to the salesperson.

3. **Non-recoverable Draw:** This is a fixed amount of money that is paid within a specified time period. Just like with a Recoverable Draw, if the actual commissions earned during a time period exceed the draw amount, the salesperson is paid the difference. However, if

the actual commissions earned during the time period do not equal or exceed the draw amount, the salesperson does not owe the company the difference. The slate is wiped clean at the beginning of the next time period.

Tables 6 and 7 demonstrate the difference between a Recoverable Draw and a Non-recoverable Draw:

Table 6: Recoverable Draw Example

Time Period	Draw Paid	Actual Commissions	Owed to Company	Commission Paid	Total Earnings
Month 1	$3,000	$4,000	-	$1,000	$4,000
Month 2	$3,000	$2,000	($1,000)	-	$3,000
Month 3	$3,000	$5,000	$1,000	$1,000	$4,000
TOTALS	$9,000	$11,000	-	$2,000	$11,000

Table 7: Non-recoverable Draw Example

Time Period	Draw Paid	Actual Commissions	Owed to Company	Commission Paid	Total Earnings
Month 1	$3,000	$4,000	-	$1,000	$4,000
Month 2	$3,000	$2,000	-	-	$3,000
Month 3	$3,000	$5,000	-	$2,000	$5,000
TOTALS	$9,000	$11,000	-	$3,000	$12,000

What is the difference between a Non-recoverable Draw and a Salary? The primary difference is that a Non-recoverable Draw can eliminate a potential fairness concern that can arise when companies use a Salary + Commission compensation plan. The best way to explain this fairness concern is by reviewing an example.

Assume that Sample Company has an annual revenue target for each salesperson of $1,000,000. Management is willing to pay 10 percent of this revenue ($100,000) as total annual salesperson compensation. Annual base salaries range from $40,000 to $60,000 based upon salesperson experience and need. The balance of each salesperson's compensation is commission.

If a salesperson receives a base salary of $60,000, their target annual commission compensation is $40,000. Assume that commissions are calculated by applying a *multiplier* against each dollar of revenue that the salesperson produces. To calculate the multiplier, divide the target commission compensation ($40,000) by the revenue target ($1,000,000). This produces a multiplier of .04.

If a salesperson receives a base salary of $40,000, their target annual commission compensation is $60,000. Dividing the target commission compensation ($60,000) by the revenue target ($1,000,000) produces a multiplier of .06.

Table 8 compares the earnings produced by these two compensation plans at three different levels of sales production:

Table 8: Compensation Comparison for Salary + Commission Plans

Annual Sales Volume	Multiplier	Annual Commission Earnings	Annual Salary	Total Earnings
$800,000	.06	$48,000	$40,000	$88,000
$800,000	.04	$32,000	$60,000	$92,000
$1,000,000	.06	$60,000	$40,000	$100,000
$1,000,000	.04	$40,000	$60,000	$100,000
$1,200,000	.06	$72,000	$40,000	$112,000
$1,200,000	.04	$48,000	$60,000	$108,000

As you can see, the salesperson with the higher base salary will have higher total earnings when the annual sales volume produced is less than the target of $1,000,000. Both salespeople will earn exactly the same amount if they hit the annual sales target on the nose. When production exceeds the annual sales target, the salesperson with the lower base salary will have higher total earnings.

The fairness concern is that these two salespeople can earn different amounts of compensation for selling exactly the same amount. This concern goes away when a Non-recoverable Draw is paid instead of a Salary. In a Non-recoverable Draw compensation plan, the multiplier for both salespeople would be $100,000/ $1,000,000 = .10. This multiplier would be applied against every dollar of revenue produced to calculate actual commissions for each period. The non-recoverable draw would be subtracted from each period's actual commissions, and any positive difference would be paid to the salesperson in the next period.

Under the Non-recoverable Draw model, at any level of annual production, both salespeople earn exactly the same amount...*as long as* their monthly production exceeds their non-recoverable draw amount. If actual commissions are lower than the non-recoverable draw by large amounts or with any regularity, the fairness concern will be resurrected, as the individual with the higher draw will show higher annual earnings. The risk of this occurring can be dramatically reduced by management inspecting salesperson *activity* on a regular basis (see Chapter 14: Inspect Activity, Not Just Results).

Additional Incentives

Companies may also add additional incentives to sales compensation plans. Common incentives include offering fixed dollar bonuses or multiplier "kickers" to promote team selling, cross-selling, sales of specific products, and increases in customer satisfaction. These incentives can motivate desirable behavior in *some* circumstances (see Chapter 13: Why Incentives Fail), but this motivation comes at the price of adding complexity to the sales compensation plan. When sales compensation plans become so complex that salespeople cannot *rapidly* calculate how their performance impacts compensation, the plan loses much of its motivational value.

Management should carefully consider which behaviors they wish to promote via sales compensation plans. They should consider the question, "Are these behaviors truly *critical* to our sales goals, or to other strategic goals?" If management decides that there are indeed multiple behaviors that should be promoted via the sales compensation plan, they should consider providing some type of "compensation calculator" to their salespeople. This calculator could take the form of a spreadsheet that enables salespeople to enter a handful of numbers and instantaneously calculate compensation. A compensation calculator will also come in handy when sales managers are explaining the compensation plan to sales candidates or new sales team members.

The Best Compensation Plan for YOUR Company

There is no such thing as a universal "best" sales compensation plan. The best plan for *your* company will be one that successfully motivates desired behaviors and is relatively easy for your salespeople to understand.

CHAPTER 13

WHY INCENTIVES FAIL

The failure of incentives is usually due to one of three conditions. The most common condition is a lack of the attributes required for sales success. When salespeople lack the attributes required for sales success, no amount of incentives will cause them to suddenly sell more effectively. A more likely outcome is that they will start to press harder to close sales and suffer a *decline* in sales performance.

If salespeople have the attributes required for sales success, the performance impact of incentives will vary based upon the weighting of selected attributes. For salespeople who are somewhat weak in the attributes of Sales Drive, Assertiveness, Energy, and Independence (i.e., they are *externally* motivated), an incentive program may indeed produce a spike in performance. However, for salespeople that are *internally* motivated, an incentive program may simply compensate them twice for doing what they would have done anyway.

A much more important issue for companies to consider when dealing with internally motivated sales-people is to ensure they don't provide performance *disincentives*. The concept of a disincentive is best illustrated with an example.

Some years ago I had a lady friend whose husband worked for a large textile manufacturer. This textile manufacturer had a policy that capped salesperson earnings at 200 percent of their annual target. My friend's husband was an exceptional salesperson, and in the second month of the fiscal year he closed the largest order in the company's history. One undesirable outcome of this achievement was that he had maximized his earning potential for the year...with ten months remaining! He did not know what to do. Clearly he had little incentive to sell for those ten months. He went to his manager, and together they tried to convince the company to change its policy, but to no avail. This very successful salesperson ended up leaving the textile manufacturer and finding another (much more lucrative) sales job.

The moral of this story is that companies should identify and eliminate performance disincentives as the first step in developing an incentive plan. The second step should be analyzing the makeup of their sales staff. How many of the salespeople have the attributes required for sales success? How many are internally motivated versus externally motivated? An incentive program will have the most impact when a significant proportion of a company's salespeople *have* the attributes required for sales success *and* they are externally motivated.

CHAPTER 14

INSPECT ACTIVITY,
NOT JUST RESULTS

Are you feeling a little nervous about building an Income Floor into your sales compensation plan? If you are, it is probably due to past bad experiences. Many companies have invested huge sums in salesperson salaries, draws, guaranteed commissions, etc., only to see their investments fail miserably. Earlier in the book we examined one of the key reasons behind these failures: hiring salespeople who lack the attributes required for sales success. This chapter will focus on a second key reason: focusing inspection on *results* rather than *activities*.

When salespeople produce results, it makes perfect sense to inspect those results. You can do so by asking questions such as: How much revenue is each salesperson producing? How profitable is that revenue? How does each salesperson's performance rate when compared against quota? How does it rate when compared against the performance of other sales team members? And so forth.

What do you do if you don't like the answers to these "results inspection" questions? What do you do when a salesperson shows some flashes of ability, but their performance is inconsistent? How do you determine what the problem(s) might be? For that matter, how do you determine whether a brand new salesperson is performing enough of the right activities to meet the thirty-, sixty-, and ninety-day performance goals that you have established for them?

To answer these questions, managers need to inspect their salespeople's *activities*. Activity inspection provides an early warning system for many performance problems. Plus, when activity is inspected regularly and consistently, it helps create and reinforce the company's sales culture.

What is activity inspection? It is the process of inspecting a salesperson's day-to-day activities to determine: (1) whether they are performing the correct *quantity* of activities; and (2) whether they are performing the activities correctly *(quality)*.

Inspecting Activity Quantity

To determine whether salespeople are investing their time in the correct activities, review their daily calendars on a regular basis. Are they performing all of the activities that are listed in their Prospecting Plans? (See Chapter 8: How to Develop an Effective Prospecting Plan.) What proportion of their time are they investing in each activity? What *quantity* of each activity are they performing?

Many salespeople don't have an effective means of tracking their daily activities in enough detail to provide accurate answers to these questions. One way to solve this problem is by using an activity-tracking form. To construct an activity-tracking form, begin by listing key daily activities in the left-hand column of a worksheet. Then, put the days of the week across the top.

Be sure to break activities down into a sufficient number of steps to make meaningful data analysis possible. For example, if you want to determine why a salesperson's cold calls are not producing the desired number of appointments, include the following activities in the tracking form: (1) the number of times the salesperson *dials* the phone; (2) the number of times they actually *talk* to someone; and (3) the number of *appointments* they book. Inspect each of these activities in sequence, and look at the ratios between the numbers. If the salesperson is only making two "dials" a day, the problem is pretty obvious. If the number of dials is acceptable, but the salesperson is not getting enough "talks" or "appointments," they may need to improve their cold-calling script, or practice to make their delivery more natural.

Each time a salesperson performs any of the activities that are listed on their tracking form, they should make a tick mark in the appropriate box. At the end of the day or week, they should total up the tick marks. The data produced by this simple discipline can be a great aid in troubleshooting performance issues.

Are you thinking, "I won't be able to get my salespeople to fill out an activity-tracking form"? If your sales compensation plan is 100-percent commission, you are probably right. However, if your sales compensation plan includes some type of income floor, then you have every right to hold your salespeople accountable for completing a tracking form. After all, how much time does it take to make a tick mark in a box? If a salesperson makes fifty tick marks a day, how much of their time is consumed by making tick marks? The value to both management *and* salespeople of the information collected via activity-tracking forms far outweighs the time cost of completing the forms.

Inspecting Activity Quality

To inspect whether salespeople are performing activities *correctly*, you either need to see them in action, or you need to conduct post-activity inspections. To see your salespeople in action, go on "buddy calls" with them. Listen in on the telephone when they are speaking with suspects, prospects, and customers. Sit in the audience when they are delivering speeches or presentations. Go to networking events together.

Post-activity inspection consists of asking detailed questions about completed activities. For example, you can ask a salesperson to explain what they did during a sales call, how they did it, and how their suspect/prospect/customer responded. Another form of post-activity inspection is performing pipeline reviews. When you inspect each opportunity in a salesperson's pipeline and ask them to justify the confidence percentages that they have assigned to opportunity line items, you will gain valuable perspective into how effectively they are performing key sales-related activities.

CHAPTER 15

WHY MOST SALES TRAINING PROGRAMS FAIL

What constitutes failure in a sales training program? A sales training program is considered a failure if the salespeople who completed the program are unable to integrate the concepts taught during the training into their day-to-day selling activities.

Such failures are frustrating for both employers and salespeople. Employers are frustrated because they don't earn the returns they expect from their training investments. Salespeople are frustrated because they feel that the time spent attending training was wasted.

Why do sales training programs fail? Some fail because the content is poorly designed, or because the trainer does a poor job of delivering the content. However, valid, well-designed training programs also fail. This chapter explores four reasons why these valid sales training programs fail.

Training Students Who Are Incapable of Learning

How can a sales training program be effective if the attendees lack the attributes required for sales success? Putting individuals who lack the necessary attributes through a sales training program is a little like using a brick to absorb water. Over long periods of time, the brick may actually absorb a little water. However, it won't absorb anywhere near as much water as a sponge.

Before a company invests in training its salespeople, it should determine whether each salesperson has the attributes required for sales success. Salespeople with the necessary attributes are much more likely to absorb sales training content and apply it effectively in the field. Successful application of sales training concepts in the field generates higher sales and produces the desired return on training investments. This approach also avoids wasting sales training dollars on individuals who are incapable of learning the curriculum. Increased sales minus lower training expenses equals a maximum return on training investments.

"One Size Fits All" Training Curriculums

Many sales training curriculums provide the same content at the same pace to all training attendees. There are two primary challenges with this approach. The first challenge is that individual salespeople have different training needs. The second challenge is that people learn at different rates.

To better understand the first challenge, different training needs, consider the following example. Two salespeople, Beth and Bill, work for the same company. Beth is weak in Sales Drive, which makes her reluctant to ask for orders. Bill is weak in Emotional Toughness. This makes him sensitive to rejection and limits his prospecting effectiveness. If both of these salespeople complete a generalized sales skills training course, how much improvement in sales performance should their company expect to see?

The answer is little or none. These salespeople have completely different training needs that are not best addressed by generalized sales skills training. Beth would benefit most from attending an assertiveness training class, in addition to receiving coaching to help her recognize that failing to ask for orders denies her customers valuable solutions to costly business problems. Bill needs to learn to not take rejection personally. He might also benefit from attending a class that teaches positive thinking and other motivational techniques. Unfortunately, unless their company is aware of their very specific training needs and uses *targeted* training to address them, it shouldn't expect much performance improvement.

The second challenge, differences in Learning Rates, was explored in Chapter 3. Do you remember the bucket/milk jug example? When people learn at different rates, but they are taught at the same rate, frustration is usually the outcome. Slower learners become frustrated because they can't keep up. Faster learners become frustrated because they get bored.

This doesn't mean that companies should never put their entire sales team through the same training curriculum. If an entirely new skill is being taught, such as a technique for prospecting to C-level executives, a standardized training curriculum may be entirely appropriate. However, individual learning rates should still be given careful consideration. If training attendees are grouped by learning rate and taught in separate sessions, the pace of curriculum delivery can be tailored to each group. If circumstances require all participants to be trained in a single group, slower learners should be given the opportunity to participate in voluntary extra sessions. Either approach will provide all participants with an opportunity to learn at a pace that is comfortable for them, maximizing their absorption of training content...and thereby maximizing training ROI!

Excessive Focus on Technical Details

Many managers and salespeople hold the opinion that salespeople need to have a thorough technical understanding of an offering in order to sell it effectively. To develop this understanding, companies invest substantial amounts of time and money in exhaustive training to educate salespeople on product features, performance characteristics, industry information, pricing guidelines, promotional activities, available collateral material, etc. Unfortunately, when salespeople leave these training sessions, they usually have no idea how to actually *identify or qualify opportunities* for the offering they were just "trained to sell"! This leaves the salespeople frustrated, as they feel the time spent in training was wasted. Management is equally frustrated with their sales team's inability to gain traction with new offerings, as well as their inability to learn to sell their company's entire portfolio of offerings.

This mutual frustration is often the result of a lack of recognition of one important fact: when a salesperson identifies a qualified opportunity, there is usually no shortage of knowledgeable resources that can assist the salesperson with converting the opportunity into a sale. These resources may include technical or other specialists from within the salesperson's own company, or similar resources that are employed by suppliers, channel partners, etc. If a salesperson has access to internal and/or external support resources, why should they invest time learning technical details? Instead, why don't they laser-focus their learning on gaining knowledge and skills that will help them identify and qualify opportunities? These include the following:

1. **Product/Solution/Service Overview:** What does the offering do? (in plain English)

2. **Differentiation:** What are some key differences between this particular offering and competitive offerings?

3. **Business Problems:** What business problems does the offering solve?

4. **Qualifying Questions:** What questions should a salesperson ask to determine whether a prospect or customer has the business problems that the offering can solve, and to quantify the impact of the business problems?

5. **Available Support Resources:** What resources are available to help the salespeople manage other steps of the sales cycle, such as detailed qualification, technical qualification, configuration, quote/proposal, service delivery, etc.?

If a company has a large portfolio of offerings, they can help their salespeople "get dangerous quickly" with their entire portfolio by providing this type of summary information for each offering in a standardized format. Standardized formats enable salespeople to rapidly familiarize themselves with new offerings. Plus, "get dangerous quickly" documents make handy cheat sheets for salespeople to take with them on sales calls.

A sample "get dangerous quickly" document is provided in Appendix B.

Lack of Reinforcement Training

When companies invest in sales training, the expected outcome is often a change in their salespeople's behavior. Unfortunately, most companies drastically underestimate the amount of time and effort that must be invested to accomplish behavioral change.

Sitting in a class for a couple of hours or days is a good way to *expose* salespeople to new concepts. However, new concepts feel strange and uncomfortable, and most salespeople lack confidence in their ability to execute them correctly. Plus, they worry that attempting to use the new concepts with real, live prospects or customers will cost them sales *and* hard-won credibility. So, most salespeople abandon the new concepts and continue to rely on the behaviors that are comfortable for them.

If companies want to change their salespeople's behavior, the management team (from top executives to individual sales managers) must make a different level of commitment to training. The concepts taught during a training class must be *repeated* and *reinforced* on a regular, consistent basis. The salespeople must also be provided with a nonthreatening environment where they can repeatedly practice the new concepts until they become second nature.

If a company is willing to invest in "train-the-trainer" training for its sales managers, the sales managers *may* be able to conduct effective reinforcement training. However, there are some challenges with this approach. First, not every sales manager has the attributes required for success as a trainer. Second, learning the new concepts well enough to teach them effectively may require a larger investment of time and effort than the sales managers feel they can afford to make. Third, because of their busy schedules, it may be difficult for the sales managers to deliver reinforcement training with the frequency and consistency necessary to accomplish behavioral change. If any of these conditions exist, the company should consider contracting with an outside service to provide reinforcement training.

AFTERWORD

TAKING THE NEXT STEP

Congratulations! You have completed *How to Beat the 80/ 20 Rule in Selling*. I hope you feel you have a better understanding of what it takes to succeed in sales, build top-performing sales teams, and resolve inconsistent sales performance. Armed with this knowledge, what is your next step?

If You Are Considering a Career in Sales

Before you quit your current job and pursue a career in sales, wouldn't you like to know whether you have the attributes required for sales success? 80/20 Performance, Inc. can help you answer this crucial question. We have created a special service bundle for the readers of this book. This service bundle includes the online assessments that we use to measure the attributes required for sales success, plus a thirty-minute telephone consultation. If you would like more information, please visit the 80/20 Performance, Inc. website: www.8020performance.com, or call (866) 531-3917.

If You Are a Business Owner, Executive, or Manager

If you are a business owner, executive, or manager, 80/20 Performance, Inc. has an offer for you, too. If you would like to increase the proportion of top performers on your sales team and/or improve the performance of existing sales team members, give us a call at (866) 531-3917. We will schedule a free telephone consultation to discuss your specific situation.

Speeches, Seminars, and Workshops

If you are interested in having Alan Rigg address your organization, or if you would like to receive information on seminars and workshops, give us a call at (866) 531-3917. You can also contact us via e-mail: info@8020performance.com, or visit our website: www.8020performance.com.

Best wishes for sales success!

APPENDIX A

SAMPLE M-A-I-N BP QUALIFICATION DOCUMENT

All prospects are *not* created equal. Salespeople need to help prospects explore whether their business problems are substantial enough to justify investing time in a sales cycle (Business Problem Qualification). However, salespeople *also* need to determine whether the prospect is worthy of time and resource investments by the salesperson's company. If a prospect is not a good fit, a wise salesperson disengages from the opportunity (why not refer them to a competitor and let the competitor burn some cycles?) and searches for other prospects.

A sample M-A-I-N BP Qualification Document is provided on the following pages. This document includes questions that will help salespeople avoid being blindsided by issues that can delay sales cycles or even destroy opportunities outright.

The acronym M-A-I-N BP stands for:

- Money

- Authority

- Information

- Need

- Buying Process

Sample M-A-I-N BP Qualification Document

Money

- How will they pay for a solution?
- Has a budget been established?
- Are they credit worthy?

Authority

- Who needs to approve an acquisition of this nature?

Information

- What information do the decision-makers require before they can make a decision?
- What format does this information need to be in?

Need

- What is the business case supporting a positive acquisition decision?
- How compelling is it? In other words, can we *quantify* (i.e., associate dollars with) the pain the prospect is feeling?
- Is this quantified business impact substantial enough to warrant investment by the prospect's organization *and our company* in identifying and fixing the problem(s)?

Buying **P**rocess

- What is the prospect's company's buying (procurement) process?
- What impact might this process have on the profitability of the transaction?
- What competitive advantage will we receive if we invest our time and resources in designing a solution?

NOTES:

1. If you don't know the answers to **ALL** of the above questions, it is highly likely you are wasting time and resources.

2. **Opportunity qualification is not a one-time process.** As an opportunity progresses through the sales cycle, you should frequently ask whether any of the answers to the qualification questions have changed. If an answer changes, it will probably impact the length of the sales cycle and may even destroy the viability of the opportunity. At minimum, an answer change will probably require a change in focus and/or a reprioritization of planned activities.

3. **Never feel bad about disqualifying an opportunity.** The amount of opportunity in each territory is virtually unlimited. If you carefully qualify and re-qualify each opportunity, and only invest time and resources in qualified opportunities, you will *maximize* your return on time and resources invested.

APPENDIX B

SAMPLE "GET DANGEROUS QUICKLY" DOCUMENT

If a company has a large portfolio of offerings, they can help their salespeople "get dangerous quickly" with their entire portfolio by providing summary information for each offering in a **standardized format**. Standardized formats enable salespeople to rapidly familiarize themselves with new offerings. Plus, "get dangerous quickly" documents make handy cheat sheets for salespeople to take on sales calls.

A sample "get dangerous quickly" document is provided on the following pages. This document includes the following components:

1. **Overview:** What does the offering do (in plain English)?

2. **Differentiation:** What are some key differences between this offering and competitive offerings?

3. **Business Problems:** What business problems does the offering solve?

4. **Qualifying Questions:** What questions should a salesperson ask to determine whether a prospect or customer has the business problems that the offering can solve, and to quantify the impact of these business problems?

Sample "Get Dangerous Quickly" Document

Supplier: BMC

General Category: Storage Management

Function: Relational Database Backup and Restore

Product Name: SQL-BackTrack

Overview/Differentiation	Business Problems	Qualifying Questions
Intelligent tool that simplifies and automates many tasks associated with backup and recovery of relational databases. Provides a higher level of functionality than available from other data protection products and/or native tools bundled with databases. Key features: · Guided recovery · Minimized recovery "think time" and errors · Right-sized recovery (recover only what you need, when you need it) · Flexible, high-performance backup · Enterprise Snapshot for UNIX ("instant" backup) · Manage multiple, heterogeneous databases from a central GUI	· Many mission-critical applications (e-business, manufacturing, point-of-sale, etc.) need to access relational databases in order to function. If a database has problems (goes down or suffers data loss or corruption), application downtime can cost companies tens of thousands of dollars per minute in lost sales, lost customers, and lost opportunities. · Database backup and recovery is a complex and error-prone process. This conflicts with the need for speedy recovery from failure, especially in high-availability environments.	· What is your cost of downtime? · How critical are your databases to your business? · What is your time to recover (TTR) if a database goes down? · How fast are your databases growing? · Have you ever had a database failure you couldn't recover from? How about a failure that took "too long" to recover from? How did these failures impact your business? · How often do your database recoveries fail and need to be started over again?

Supplier: BMC

General Category: Storage Management

Product Name: SQL-BackTrack

Function: Relational Database Backup and Restore

Overview/Differentiation	Business Problems	Qualifying Questions
Here is how SQL-BackTrack assists with each step of the database recovery process: • **Analysis:** Auto-discovery tells DBA what is missing from the database • **Source:** Historical backup management keeps track of backups and determines source for data to be restored • **Preparation:** Issues appropriate commands needed to prepare database for the recovery process • **Restore:** Copies backup data from source to correct destination • **Recover:** Issues appropriate commands in correct sequence • **Post-Recovery Clean-Up:** Performs or advises DBA on appropriate post-recovery clean-up process, ensuring the database is ready to resume full operation	• File system backup tools have no intelligence concerning how files go together to build more complex structures such as databases. As a result, significant manual intervention is required to restore databases, lengthening database and application downtime and increasing related financial losses. • DBAs may write scripts for database backups. This makes backups dependent upon the DBA. If the DBA is out of the business or leaves the company, the company's ability to backup and restore their databases is at risk. Plus, while backups can be scripted, it is very difficult to script recoveries. **Note:** According to Gartner, only 20% of outages requiring recovery are due to physical failures, while 80% are due to human error.	• How often do you need to recover just a few database objects instead of an entire database? • How many database servers do you have? Are they centralized or distributed? • What applications do you plan to introduce that might demand a more robust database backup/recovery scheme? • Are you using native database tools (RMAN, EBU, ONbar) for database backup and recovery? How happy are you with these tools? • How much DBA turnover do you have? How does this impact your backup coverage?

APPENDIX C

SUGGESTED READING

Adler, L. *Hire With Your Head: Using POWER Hiring To Build Great Companies.* Hoboken, New Jersey: John Wiley & Sons, 2002.

Buckingham, M. and C. Coffman. *First, Break All The Rules: What The World's Greatest Managers Do Differently.* New York: Simon & Schuster, 1999.

Buckingham, M. and D. O. Clifton, PhD. *Now, Discover Your Strengths.* New York: The Free Press, 2001.

Gitomer, J. *The Sales Bible: The Ultimate Sales Resource, Revised Edition.* Hoboken, New Jersey: John Wiley & Sons, 2003.

Greenberg, H., H. Weinstein, and P. Sweeney. *How to Hire & Develop Your Next Top Performer: The Five Qualities That Make Salespeople Great.* New York: McGraw-Hill, 2001.

Parinello, A. *Selling to VITO: The Very Important Top Officer.* Holbrook, Massachusetts: Adams Media Corporation, 1999.

Sandler, D. *You Can't Teach a Kid to Ride a Bike at a Seminar.* United States of America: Bay Head Publishing, Inc., 2000.

Sherman, D. *The Networking Guy's Top 50 Tips: A Simple Guide to Networking Success.* Scottsdale, Arizona: The Networking Guy LLC, 2003.

INDEX

A

Account penetration, 28
Activity inspection
  definition, 100
  importance of, 100
  quality inspection, 102
    buddy calls, 102
    post-activity inspec-
      tion, 102
  quantity inspection, 100
    activity tracking
      form, 101
Assessments
  behavioral tests, 7
  modern assessment
    technologies, 7, 18
  personality profiles, 7
  special offer, 113
  statistics, 16
Attributes
  critical
    emotional tough-
      ness, 20
    reasoning ability, 20

sales drive, 19
service drive, 21
for success in
  management, 41
  training, 111
job specific, 35
  career path, 40
  communication, 39
  field service, 40
  geography, 36
  hunter, farmer or hy-
    brid, 37
  manageability, 40
  nature of the cus-
    tomer 35
  nature of the offer-
    ing, 36
  prospecting, 38
  sales environment,
    36
  sales style, 37
  support resources, 39
  training, 40
other important

To order additional copies of
How to Beat the 80/20 Rule in Selling,
visit these fine online bookstores:

www.amazon.com
www.barnesandnoble.com
www.booksamillion.com
www.borders.com

80/20 Performance, Inc.

P.O. Box 8772
Scottsdale, AZ 85252-8772
Toll Free: (866) 531-3917
Fax: (866) 531-3917
www.8020performance.com
info@8020performance.com

Printed in the United Kingdom
by Lightning Source UK Ltd.
101536UKS00001B/64